MASTERING
PRACTICE
GROWTH

MASTERING PRACTICE GROWTH

The
DEFINITIVE GUIDE TO GROWING
Your Dental Practice or Dental Group

IAN McNICKLE

Advantage.

Published by Advantage, Charleston, South Carolina.
Member of Advantage Media Group.

ADVANTAGE is a registered trademark, and the Advantage colophon is a trademark of Advantage Media Group, Inc.

Printed in the United States of America.

10 9 8 7 6 5 4 3 2 1

ISBN: 978-1-64225-099-2
LCCN: 2019913504

Cover design by Megan Elger.
Layout design by Wesley Strickland

This publication is designed to provide accurate and authoritative information in regard to the subject matter covered. It is sold with the understanding that the publisher is not engaged in rendering legal, accounting, or other professional services. If legal advice or other expert assistance is required, the services of a competent professional person should be sought.

Advantage Media Group is proud to be a part of the Tree Neutral® program. Tree Neutral offsets the number of trees consumed in the production and printing of this book by taking proactive steps such as planting trees in direct proportion to the number of trees used to print books. To learn more about Tree Neutral, please visit www.treeneutral.com.

Advantage Media Group is a publisher of business, self-improvement, and professional development books and online learning. We help entrepreneurs, business leaders, and professionals share their Stories, Passion, and Knowledge to help others Learn & Grow. Do you have a manuscript or book idea that you would like us to consider for publishing? Please visit advantagefamily.com or call 1.866.775.1696.

CONTENTS

A s CEO of a dental corporate incubator and accelerator, growth has always been a critical focus. To provide that capability it was necessary to find best-of-class business partners to assist me in offering expertise in all areas that a business requires to be successful. That journey meant finding individuals who could provide expertise in online and traditional marketing, social media, website development, finance, accounting, operational strategy and execution, information technology, personnel development, and most importantly overall management direction. As you would expect, these areas relate 100 percent to the day-to-day needs of growing and managing a modern dental practice as well.

My past includes starting a practice from scratch that ultimately grew to a multispecialty practice with ten doctors and twenty-five team members. Those years presented continuous challenges as we ran into constant barriers and plateaus. We worked very hard and frequently experimented to finally break through. It took many years to learn all those lessons. I truly wish I had then what is provided to you now in the pages of this book.

As dentists, you are the CEOs of your own businesses and are constantly challenged to find valuable resources to provide the necessary expertise to stay on top in this fast-paced, constantly changing business environment. Just a few years ago, did we ever think we would need to understand search engine optimization and Google algorithms in order to grow our practices?

This book provides you with not only critical tools to maximize success but also, just as important in my opinion, direct connections to the leadership in the areas necessary to compete and succeed in the modern dental landscape.

Ian McNickle is truly one of the most prominent thought leaders in our industry today. Over the years, I've seen him coach and educate hundreds of dentists with an uncanny ability to explain highly technical topics in a manner that is easy to understand. He has a unique grasp of high-level strategy and detailed technical knowledge across a wide range of topics. Dentistry is fortunate to have him given the content and contacts he has provided us in the pages ahead.

Dr. Lou Shuman, DMD, CAGS

Founder and CEO of Cellerant Consulting Group

T he dental industry has undergone a major transformation over the last few decades. In years past, patient referrals and phone book listings were all you needed to maintain a healthy, thriving practice. Insurance reimbursements were pretty good, and marketing simply wasn't all that necessary. Many of the dentists I speak with across the country from the boomer generation often refer to that period as the golden age of dentistry. In their opinion, it was more cordial, easier to maintain a profitable practice, and in a sense, a simpler time.

As time rolled on, the digital era began to take shape. The rise of the internet changed nearly every aspect of modern civilization, and dentistry was no different. All of a sudden, patients could simply go online and search for a dentist. In fact, they could search for dentists specializing in certain procedures, dentists who took a specific insurance, dentists who offered new patient specials, dentists who were located closest to them, and so on. Potential patients could also read online reviews to judge a practice without ever talking to a single human being. At the same time, the ongoing decline in insurance reimbursements chipped away at margins on a large segment of the patient base. In direct response to these factors, marketing began to become more important, and many dentists looked to purchase their first websites.

Then came the period of "irrational exuberance," as Warren Buffett would later call it. The Great Recession of 2008–09 rocked the economy to its core, and many industries were in outright panic mode. Fortunately, dentistry fared better than most industries, but it was still hit pretty hard. Patient counts dropped for many dentists, as did elective procedures with higher margins. To make matters worse, insurance reimbursement rates continued their decline. As a result, many dentists who had been counting down to their retirement were forced to put their plans on hold indefinitely.

Two major trends emerged in the postrecession period to significantly shape dentistry: (1) general dentists started performing a lot more specialty procedures, and (2) the rise of dental support organizations (DSOs) changed the competitive landscape in a big way.

Feeling the pinch from the Great Recession, general dentists began referring out fewer patients as they did more dentistry in house, creating a resulting ripple effect felt to this day by specialists. Oral surgeons and periodontists were getting fewer referrals for dental implants, orthodontists were getting fewer referrals for orthodontics, and so on. The net effect was that general dentists wanted to do more marketing to get the word out about their expanded array of service offerings, and many specialists had to start marketing for the first time.

During this same transition period, another disruptive force was shaking up industry dynamics as DSOs gained momentum in their continuing march toward industry consolidation. DSOs have many advantages over individual practices. They can generate impressive economies of scale that allow them to centralize the business aspects of a dental practice such as management, purchasing, billing, human resources (HR), marketing, information technology (IT), finance, and related functions. These jobs are typically performed by people with specific training in these areas so not only do DSOs have an efficiency advantage but also an expertise advantage. These people

So where does that leave us? How does the modern dentist compete?

are normally better at their jobs since they have specific education and experience in these areas and focus solely on the specific job function. Size also provides leverage for negotiating with vendors for more favorable pricing.

So where does that leave us? How does the modern dentist compete? What options and tools are available to help them navigate this supercompetitive landscape?

Those questions are at the heart of this book's genesis. Having personally researched more than one hundred companies over the last several years, my aim is to provide comprehensive information and a set of resources to help all dentists improve and grow their practices. In my opinion, the companies recommended in this book are exceptionally good at what they do, and in most cases, they are considered the best in their category. The criteria for companies to be included in this book are that (1) the companies must have significant dental industry knowledge, (2) the companies must have a long track record of proven results over time, (3) the companies must have a good reputation and treat their clients in an honest and ethical manner, and (4) I was able to verify their claims with independent references.

In full disclosure, some of these companies have financially contributed to the cost of helping me write and publish this book. However, financial contributions had no impact on my decision to include these companies in the book, as the decision was made solely on the four criteria listed previously. Indeed, many companies that wanted to be included in this book were not based on those criteria. I will not be compensated by the recommended companies for any sales that may result from this book (with the exception of the two companies I co-own: WEO Media and The DSO Project).

While some readers of this book will take advantage of the information it contains to make huge improvements to their existing practices, other readers will take the opportunity to the next level and scale to multiple locations and beyond. Whatever your goals and aspirations may be, I sincerely hope you'll find this book to be an invaluable resource to aid you in your journey.

OPERATIONAL EXCELLENCE

"You cannot scale chaos."

I began my career as a process engineer in the high-tech industry, specifically in the sector of semiconductor manufacturing. Fresh out of school with a bachelor of science in mechanical engineering, I was eager to work hard and learn as much as I could. If you've never been in a high-tech fab, it is something to behold. There are people walking around in bunny suits 24/7, working in cleanrooms that are orders of magnitude cleaner than any surgical operating room. Really expensive machinery and cutting-edge measurement tools fill the bright, sterile rooms. Computers lit up with hundreds of control charts measure every detail of every process. It was a fairly intimidating environment for a young kid just out of college.

I learned many things in my ten years of working in the high-tech industry, and one of the most important lessons was this: you cannot scale chaos! An organization must achieve a minimum level of operational effectiveness before it can/should increase production. Otherwise, problems that exist at low volume will kill you at high volume. This holds true in any industry, whether it's manufacturing or service, professional or blue collar, a local business or a Fortune 500 firm.

So what do billion-dollar, semiconductor fabs have in common with dental practices? Well, actually, more than you might think. At the end of the day, operational excellence comes down to two things: people and processes. If you can get the right people on your team, then you can create the right culture. If you can create the right culture, then you can develop high-performing teams. However, even with great people and a winning culture, you must have well-developed metrics and processes or your business is still likely to fail (or at least significantly underperform).

This opening section of the book will highlight some of the core elements needed to create operational excellence in a dental practice. Whether your goal is to create a single high-performing location, scale to multiple high-performing locations, or build a DSO, it all starts with people and processes.

Throughout this book I have invited a few industry experts to offer their sage advice and knowledge as content contributors. When it comes to building teams and implementing processes, I could think of no better firm to help than Fortune Management. As the largest practice management coaching firm in the dental industry, they have a base of collective experience that is unsurpassed. Their contributions are heavily featured in the rest of this opening section.

CULTURE: CREATING A HIGH-PERFORMING TEAM

In the dental industry, there is a huge variation in operational performance from practice to practice. According to Fortune Management, the significant difference between highly successful teams and those who are at or below average is rarely clinical talent. It's simply the discipline to live and honor codefined culture agreements. Top-notch dental teams—those who are the highest paid for the emotional and professional value they bring to each other, their patients, and the marketplace—are formed in an environment of mutual respect, safe communication, and accountability. These top-notch teams also consistently reach goals that support integrity, value, and lasting relationships. Egos are secondary where continuous practice growth, sustained practice profitability, and high compensation reside. This level of success begins and ends with a defined winning team culture.

Of course, every dental team aspires to be a winning team and to reap the rewards that come with being at the top of their game. And obviously, winning does not just miraculously happen. Instead, it takes dedication, devotion, and commitment. We believe these five fundamental elements define what is required to perform at a highly successful level:

1. **The "be" mission.** How will we serve? What values are absolute? Why are we here? How will we make a difference? This is the absolute guidepost of existence and needs to be addressed daily with emotion and energy.

2. **Culture agreements.** How will we behave in the workplace toward our team members and patients while being individually accountable? Clearly define the character, attributes, and people skills necessary to be involved in an A+ culture. Acquire and enforce them diligently.

3. **Vision.** Where specifically are we going? Where will we be? Who will be with us? What will we look like in one year, five years, and ten years? How will we be accountable? This includes daily, monthly, and yearly goals as well as regular review against these goals.

4. **Communications.** What specific communication processes are we committed to? Which tools will we use to document and communicate? These must be rehearsed and utilized consistently by all stakeholders regardless of status.

5. **Celebrations.** As goals are attained, share them generously and evenly. Play as an A+ team, learn as an A+ team, and win as an A+ team!

Indeed, a practice that embraces this approach to building culture is far more likely to achieve high performance.

AT THE HEART OF EVERY GREAT CULTURE IS A GREAT LEADER

I have been in hundreds of practices over the years, general dentistry and specialist alike. I'm often surprised when doctors complain about their staff: "Why don't they do what they're supposed to do?" or "We have a couple of people with really bad attitudes." In these situations, I always wonder what they are doing as leaders to allow such issues to fester.

What would it be like if each employee was a true team member, aligned with your vision, bought in to your culture, taking "ownership" in your business, and supporting you in reaching your goals? Fortune Management offers this advice:

As executive business coaches, we are continuously studying what makes businesses grow and prosper. One of the fundamentals is great leadership.

Having a vision and having the leader's expectations clearly defined, then having the team design and agree on codes of conduct and core values will create this environment. Still, they may not immediately turn into a great team. So the leader's next step is to elegantly hold each team member accountable, support them, and celebrate wins. When an outstanding environment and accountabilities are put into place, employees either step up to the plate or leave. We have seen mediocre employees turn into outstanding team members when the work environment is supportive. The leader's belief in each team member's desire to grow and contribute is the foundation.

In business, being a great leader and having a great team that rallies behind your vision and purpose as if it was their own creates remarkable results. So how do we become great leaders? What mind-set is the employer operating from on a regular basis? Is he thinking, "I'm just not a good leader"? Is she thinking, "That's just not me. I can't lead people"? People often attribute leadership to some sort of talent or innate ability. Fortunately, leadership is not an innate ability; it can be learned. And if we learn the belief systems and thinking of great leaders, we, too, can become great leaders.

There are many types of leadership styles such as the laissez-faire approach, the collaborative team approach, the authoritarian approach, and the transformational approach. If you think you aren't a leader, you are communicating this. Remember, you cannot not communicate. You not leading is actually leading your team to not be aligned with your vision and your purpose. No one style is the best; no one style works in all situations. In leading our own teams, we have used all styles. However, we know that we are using them deliberately to fulfill our vision. Unexamined, we are just using one style and might not be getting our desired outcomes. As you are on this journey of refining your leadership skills, you will be able to see what styles will give you the results you want.

While you are discovering (and remembering) the distinctions that make great leaders, we will tell you a few things we know help create powerful leaders. First, do you have a vision that inspires you? Get yourself totally connected to your vision every single morning; that will make your thinking consistent with your vision. If your mind focuses on what's wrong, immediately shift your thinking back to your vision. To create an environment in your practice that will make your team extraordinary, model the emotional state you want to see from your team. Share your vision, and then create it. Let them know how you are going to support that vision. How can they help fulfill it? Honor their contributions and ideas, and ask how you can support them. When people are inspired, they do amazing things. Have them be accountable to those goals and guide them toward who they will become by attaining those goals.

Our results come from our actions, which come from the mind-sets we choose on a regular basis. Our mind-sets (again, what we are thinking at any given moment) are totally shaped by the meanings we give to the things happening around us, what is provided by our belief systems. Most times, we do not recognize the mind-sets we are in. Even though you are working on becoming a great leader, unless you are conscious of it, you will revert back to your old way of thinking. What if we stopped and asked ourselves on a regular basis, What outcomes are we getting? Are they a match for our vision and goals? What mind-set would I need right now to lead my team to achieve those outcomes? What mind-set would my team have to have to achieve those outcomes?

Our definition of being a powerful leader is having the ability to consistently create your vision, purpose, and the outcomes that support that vision and purpose and the ability to influence your team to be so aligned with you that they consistently create your vision, purpose, and outcomes, taking them on as their own.

Working on a team with a clear vision, a common goal, and a common purpose is one of the most rewarding experiences an employer or employee can have. Successful leaders can make any dream or vision come true when they can hire and inspire people to align and find their own purposes in making the shared vision a reality. There's no limit to what great teams will accomplish when aligned with a common purpose and a trusted leader to guide them. On the other hand, working without a clear direction or common purpose will leave you and your team lost, dissatisfied, and frustrated.

STRUCTURE: SOURCING AND ACCOUNTABILITY

How many times have you delegated something to your office staff only to find that it didn't got done? How many times have you sat through yet another staff meeting, and although many great ideas

There is a big difference between people who do as they are told and people who, on their own, consistently and effectively do what needs to be done.

came up, nothing ever came of it? How many times have you taken responsibility for something because you felt you couldn't count on your team to follow through?

As practice owners and leaders, we want to build a team of intelligent, competent, dependable, and accountable people so that we can accomplish more in our businesses and get bigger, better results year after year. Truly one of the most frequently encountered challenges is the accountability factor.

There is a big difference between people who do as they are told and people who, on their own, consistently and effectively do what needs to be done. A culture of accountability begins with team selection. In selecting the right individuals to help you build your organization, a great attitude is a critical characteristic. Skill can be trained, but it is difficult to train attitude, and even if you can do it, it takes a long time.

The coaches at Fortune Management provide some excellent guidelines in this area:

Select people who already possess a great attitude: those who are positive, supportive, genuine, gracious, and respectful. Next, look for people who bring value to your business and are willing to grow and become better and more effective in their job field. Last, consider someone's beliefs about the role they will play, the industry itself, and the importance of their role in meeting practice goals. Some of the most important decisions you will ever make in your life are about the people who will surround you. It is true that "one bad apple can spoil the bunch," and this is especially so when it comes to team dynamics. If the bad apple has a stronger, louder voice than any other in the practice, that person will have a profoundly negative impact on you, your patients, your team, and your practice. Help that person find employment elsewhere as soon as possible. It is worth paying the unemployment tax to no longer have that individual undermining your results.

Once you have the right people, you must help them develop the skills necessary to perform their jobs to your expectations and in service to the patients and practice. The first step is to make your expectations clear and give them an example of what a great job looks, sounds, and feels like. Provide them with a written job descriptions. Give them models to follow in producing the intended result. Then stand back and let them practice, give them a little bit of room to try out the skill and use it. A Chinese proverb observes, "I hear and I forget, I see and I remember, I do and I understand." Any new team member needs the experience of doing a task to make distinctions that will improve their results the next time. Give feedback on what they are doing really well and what areas still need work, and then let them do it again. Throughout this process, you want to build competence and confidence so that they are willing and empowered to be accountable for the desired result. Offer supportive correction when they miss a step, and acknowledge them for what they are doing well.

Beginning the process of creating a culture of accountability requires only a few things from the business owner or leader. Once you have selected the right people and trained them in the skill sets they need, you must establish lines of accountability so that each of your team leaders knows where they are most needed and where they can add the most value. Establish source areas within your practice so that when challenges arise, there is someone designated to address the issue and create a solution.

There's a simple formula team members can follow to achieve specific objectives. At Fortune Management, we call it "The Ultimate Success Formula," and there are only five steps:

1.   **Be clear about your outcome.** What specific result do I want in this area, or what result best supports the practice's vision and goals?

2.   **Know your reasons why.** Why is it a must for me to achieve this outcome?

3.   **Take action and model success.** Who has gotten this result before, and what can I model in their strategy?

4.   **Monitor your results.** Track performance versus goals. Is this strategy getting me closer to my desired result?

5.   **Be flexible in your approach.** What other strategies can I leverage to get this result? What have I not thought of? Who else might have an idea to support this result? What models exist that others have used to get this result?

As you begin to see people stepping up and taking responsibility for their results and outcomes, your job as the leader is to take the stand that they are capable enough, intelligent enough, resourceful enough, and creative enough to get this result. Use morning huddles and weekly team meetings as opportunities for the designated, responsible "source" person to discuss their outcomes and their strategies. Ask them leading questions that allow them to find solutions to whatever challenges are impeding their results. Enhance their self-esteem by giving them positive feedback when things work out and by offering supportive correction when things don't. If your team members know it is okay to make a mistake, they will be more willing to put themselves on the line for results.

TRACKING PERFORMANCE

It can be difficult to know if your job performance is great, good, mediocre, or poor unless there are some clear metrics in place to help define the expectations of the job. In a dental practice, each person must do their job well if the practice is going to perform at a high level. Therefore, it is critical to have systems and tools in place to track and report each person's KPIs (key performance indicators).

Carefully think about the job description and core job functions of each person in the practice for front office staff, back office staff, hygiene staff, and doctors alike. The goal here would be to identify three to five KPIs for each person in the practice that truly impact success (however you define success based on your practice's goals and mission, vision, and values). Once you have defined the KPIs for each person, you'll need to put systems in place to track and report these KPIs. Tracking strategies are examined in detail throughout section 4.

OUTSOURCING AND HIRING EXPERTS

Now that we're all on the same page about the importance of people and processes, let's dig a bit deeper into how to truly maximize the performance of your people and processes. In any business there are core services that really define your business and your value proposition to your customers. In the case of dental practices, the core service is obviously dentistry, in particular, the care and oral health of your patients.

The clinical aspect of patient care is the most important, but there are many other touch points in the overall patient experience. How does your front office person answer the phone? Are they grumpy or polite and helpful? Is your waiting room clean and professional, or is it a bit unkempt and cluttered? Do you use modern technology or older equipment? Do you have effective methods and tools to explain treatment recommendations to your patients? Are patients often frustrated with your insurance and billing processes and/or people? Do you keep your practice safe, clean, and regulatory compliant (with the Occupational Safety and Health Administration [OSHA], the Health Insurance Portability and Accountability Act [HIPAA], etc.)? Admittedly these are not the first things most dentists think of when it comes to patient experience, but these are absolutely real reasons you can lose patients, lose referrals, and even get negative online reviews.

Of the hundreds of dental practices I've visited, the vast majority of them would greatly benefit from the expertise of people who specialize in a specific area or discipline. In fact, it is quite common for practices to hire consultants and third-party experts for specific job functions, but in my experience, this is a greatly underused strategy.

Investment in training your people and improving your processes almost always pays big dividends.

For example, think about case acceptance. Do you track case acceptance by doctor and hygienist? If so, you will notice differences between your team members. If you have high-performing people on staff, study them closely to see what they are doing, and model that behavior. However, in most cases, all team members could probably improve. In these situations, it can be valuable to hire consultants, coaches, and trainers to work with your team to improve high-impact areas such as case acceptance.

Likewise, there are many other areas, including marketing, HR, IT, accounting, and OSHA/HIPAA compliance, where it usually makes sense to solicit third-party help. Here are three highly recommended companies that currently serve thousands of dentists across the country.

SERVICE RECOMMENDATION: FORTUNE MANAGEMENT

Fortune Management is the nation's largest and most comprehensive practice management organization. Fortune currently coaches over one thousand dental clients across the country in nearly every aspect of running and optimizing a practice.

For more information, please see section 6, "Recommended Resources to Grow Your Practice."

SERVICE RECOMMENDATION: HARRIS BIOMEDICAL

Harris Biomedical is a leading dental compliance company that has advised and served over ten thousand dental practices across the country. They offer a full range of services designed to help your practice remain compliant and respond to the mandates of OSHA and HIPAA as well as health department regulations.

For more information, please see section 6, "Recommended Resources to Grow Your Practice."

SERVICE RECOMMENDATION: ACADEMY OF DENTAL CPAS

The ADCPA was founded in 2001 to organize and share best practices among dental certified public accountants (CPAs). Today there are dozens of ADCPA member firms collectively providing accounting and advisory services to over nine thousand dentists across the country. This collective knowledge base is a powerful resource for any dentist looking to make good business decisions, minimize taxes, and maximize profitability.

For more information, please see section 6, "Recommended Resources to Grow Your Practice."

EXTERNAL MARKETING FOR NEW PATIENTS

T he last decade has seen massive changes in how we reach out to potential patients. It's no longer enough to simply have a good-looking website; it's got to be ranked high on Google and be supported by glowing online reviews, engaging videos, and relevant social media.

However, the fundamental process for acquiring new patients hasn't changed. The three steps remain (1) generate a lead, (2) convert that lead into an appointment, and (3) convert that appointment into sold dentistry (i.e., case acceptance). Let's look more closely at each of these steps and how they work today.

STEP 1: GENERATING THE LEAD

In external marketing, the two primary paths to finding new patients are online marketing and direct-to-consumer (D2C) marketing. Online marketing is usually more predictable, more reliable, and more affordable—and it's also easier to track your results. D2C marketing can generate significant numbers of leads, but it can also be a huge waste of money. If you engage in D2C marketing, you can typically expect anywhere from a 1.0 to 3.0 percent response rate.

By contrast, websites typically convert 10–20 percent of the traffic into leads, and when you look at the popular review sites where people go to check your online reputation, anywhere from 40–70 percent of that traffic will convert into leads. That's why I recommend developing a robust online marketing program as your first step in external marketing; it's a more dependable and less expensive way to get traction.

LEAD CONVERSION FUNNEL

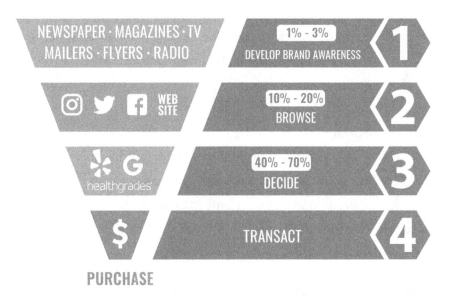

As your online marketing program begins to produce results, you'll be able to develop a baseline range for your KPIs. Typical KPIs would include website traffic, Google rankings, the number of phone calls and appointment requests generated, the number of live chat leads you get, and how many direct appointments are scheduled.

Once your practice has had time to develop that baseline tracking, you can consider introducing D2C marketing efforts if you're looking for additional new patient flow.

There are a variety of media options for D2C campaigns: direct mail postcards, radio ads, print ads, TV ads, and billboards. I generally recommend starting with one D2C campaign at a time so that you can more accurately measure the direct versus indirect responses. Direct responses would be calls to the specific tracking number used on the D2C campaign. Indirect responses would be people who saw the D2C ad and then went online to check out the practice's website, online reviews, social media, and so on and then became a lead from one of the online marketing properties. This is why you need to first establish a baseline with your online marketing metrics: when you get a spike in online marketing KPIs that correspond to the timing of your D2C campaign, you'll be able to more accurately estimate the amount of additional leads that actually came from that D2C campaign. If you don't have the online marketing baselines in place before running the D2C campaign, then it is more challenging to determine which marketing efforts are producing which results. This topic will be explored in more detail throughout section 4 of this book.

So let's start with online marketing as the first priority. Online marketing really has two primary steps:

1. drive traffic to the website and online properties, and

2. convert that traffic into leads by having people take the actions you want them to take.

Driving traffic to your website is achieved by the use of SEO (search engine optimization), PPC (pay-per-click) ads, social media, online review sites, videos, internal marketing, and other methods.

Once people arrive at your website, you'll want them to take action: to contact your office via phone, by live chat, or by filling out an appointment request or online scheduling form. These actions are called website lead conversion.

The ultimate goal of your online marketing is to drive new patients to the practice. This is achieved by maximizing traffic and optimizing lead conversion.

When potential patients are searching online, they typically view between two and five pieces of information about a practice before deciding to schedule an appointment. They may find the practice's website in a Google search and then go to the website for more information, check out the practice's Facebook page, and read a few Google reviews. Or they may take any variety of different tracks online before eventually contacting the office. This is why it is mission critical to develop a comprehensive, robust online presence. I often describe a robust online marketing program as being built on six pillars:

1. a website,
2. SEO,
3. PPC,
4. online reputation,
5. social media, and
6. videos.

While there are numerous combinations for what potential patients may view, the point is this—they are going to check out more than one source of information about your practice, so it is extremely important that all six pillars of your online marketing program are solid. Any weak spots mean you'll certainly lose patients to practices with a more robust online presence.

PILLAR 1: PRACTICE WEBSITE

The first pillar of your online marketing program is the practice's website, the hub of your online presence. While the finer points of developing a powerful practice website could make up an entire book, for the purposes of this one, I'm going to keep it brief.

First, there are two distinct audiences for websites: people and search engines. People respond to things such as design, layout, aesthetics, ease of use, and related factors. Google isn't interested in those and has a very different set of items it values. I'll cover this in more detail in the SEO section (under the second pillar).

Mobile optimized. Your website must be mobile responsive and optimized for mobile device screen sizes. While most newer websites are built to be mobile optimized, check to make sure yours works as well on a smartphone and tablet as it does on a desktop. Based on my analysis of hundreds of dental websites, the average website traffic from mobile devices is between 50 and 70 percent, so this isn't something you want to ignore. To check the mobile compatibility of your website, log on to Google and do a search for "Google mobile friendly test." Simply click on the test link, and enter your website address. Google will tell you if your website passes or fails. You may want to consult a website professional to understand the details behind the analysis, but you can at least get the high-level result this way.

Engaging content. This should go without saying, but most websites settle for subpar content. Your practice's website should have engaging, educational content about your doctor(s), pictures of your doctor(s) and staff, and great descriptions of your services including images and educational videos. Likewise, a practice overview video on your home page will significantly increase user engagement.

Optimized to convert leads. There are many factors that determine a website's ability to convince potential patients to contact your practice. Your website should be built with modern design techniques: it needs to have clear calls to action, include a practice overview video on the home page, feature actual photos of the practice (avoid stock photos if possible), be easy to navigate, contain educational information about the services offered, and include contact information with the phone number at the top of every page. Using 24/7 live chat and appointment request forms is also very helpful for lead conversion.

Hypertext Transfer Protocol Secure. It is becoming more important to make sure your website is secure by adding a security certificate. This will change your website address from http to https (with the *s* meaning secure). Google has indicated it wants all websites to migrate to https eventually, so it is a good idea to get out ahead of the shift and do it now so that your Google rankings don't get penalized in the future.

SERVICE RECOMMENDATION: WEO MEDIA

WEO Media builds beautiful, high-quality, professionally designed, https-secure, mobile-optimized websites for all budgets, including custom and semicustom options.

For more information, please see section 6, "Recommended Resources to Grow Your Practice."

PILLAR 2:
SEARCH ENGINE OPTIMIZATION

The second pillar of online marketing is SEO, the ongoing process of optimizing both on- and off-page factors to achieve high search result rankings on Google and other search engines. The higher your website ranks, the more website visits you'll get, which translates into more new patient leads. Google's search algorithm is believed to analyze over two hundred factors to determine how high (or low) to rank your practice's website in a search result. For clarity's sake, I find it useful to group many of these two-hundred-plus SEO factors into six major groups: website content, website code, backlinks to the website, directories, online reviews, and social media.

WEBSITE CONTENT

There are three important content strategies you can use to significantly improve your website's Google rankings. The first is using unique content as opposed to stock or duplicate content. Unique content is written specifically for your website and does not exist on any other website. Stock or duplicate content is simply content used by website companies across numerous client websites. Google places a high priority on unique content, so implementing unique content is one of the first things I recommend to clients as part of their SEO programs.

The second content strategy to improve your Google rankings is having just one topic per page. Too often dental websites feature a laundry list of services provided (e.g., crowns, bridges, veneers, implants, etc.). For people visiting the website, that list approach works fine because we understand the context. However, Google much prefers having dedicated topics on each page, so to improve your Google rankings, have at least one dedicated web page for each dental service (and dental term) you want to rank for, and of course each web page should have unique content.

The third content strategy is to have detailed FAQ pages that answer the most commonly asked questions you get. In particular, be sure to include plenty of FAQs related to the services you want to rank highly for, such as dental implants, orthodontics, cosmetic dentistry, sleep dentistry, etc. As with dental services, each FAQ should have its own dedicated web page to improve Google rankings.

WEBSITE CODE

While people see your website's graphics, colors, images, and videos, Google and other search engines see the website's HTML, otherwise known as website code. This HTML code makes up the website and tells Google all the details of how to display and format the website: its dimensions, its functionality, its mobile display, and dozens of specifics Google wants to know. In terms of what matters for SEO, there are certain items in the code that are crucial if you want to rank highly on Google. Here are some of the most fundamental and important items:

- **Title tag.** This tells the search engine the title (and often the main topic) of the web page. This often includes the primary search keyword you would like to rank for. The title tag is also the main headline that is shown on a Google search result.

- **Meta description tag.** This short sentence describes what content is on the web page and informs Google what you would like it to rank for. The meta description tag is also the text that is shown on a Google search result page below the main title of the search result. This is the supporting text to educate the person browsing the search results so they can quickly learn more about your practice.

- **Meta keyword tags.** This is typically a short list of specific keywords that you would like the specific web page to rank for.

- **Alt tags.** These tags are applied to images on your website to tell the search engines what the image is about and the relevant search terms for which you would like it to rank.

- **Schema markup code.** This code helps search engines better understand important information about your website and return more informative results to people searching for your type of business.

Note: Each web page on your website should have all these code items optimized specifically for the content on that page (meaning this needs to be done for every page, not just once for the entire website).

WEBSITE BACKLINKS (A.K.A. INCOMING LINKS)

A backlink is a link that exists on another website that links back to your website. For example, maybe your local component dental society has a list of dentists in the area, and under your practice listing, there's a link that goes back to your website. Google values backlinks to a website as a significant SEO factor. In particular, the number of backlinks, the relevance of those backlinks, the domain authority/ website traffic of the website providing the backlink, and the text in the link itself are all factors that affect your Google rankings and SEO performance.

While building backlinks is among the more difficult SEO tasks to do, it can be well worth the effort if you are able to generate more backlinks than other dental websites in your area. In my experience analyzing hundreds of dental websites, the average dental website has fewer than ten quality incoming links, so try to get at least ten or twenty incoming links as part of your SEO program. Traction in this area could be the nudge that convinces Google to push your website on to page one.

ONLINE DIRECTORIES

There are literally hundreds of online directories and business review sites that list business information such as your name, address, and phone number (commonly referred to as NAP). Search engines look at this information as part of their analysis of your practice. If a search engine finds inconsistencies in your NAP such as an old address, the wrong suite number, or even a DDS (doctor of dental surgery) instead of a DMD (doctor of dental medicine), then there is a good chance your search rankings will greatly suffer. This is because the search engine knows something is incorrect, but doesn't necessarily know what is incorrect, so it will typically push your search rankings way down since it doesn't want to display false information to people using the search engine. This is why one of the very first things I recommend after a website launches is correcting all these directories as quickly as possible.

ONLINE REVIEWS

In the dental industry, I often talk about the "Big Four" review sites: Google, Facebook, Yelp, and Healthgrades. The topic of online reputation will be covered in more detail later in this section, but as online reviews pertain to SEO rankings, there are several key elements you'll want to focus on:

- **Quantity of reviews.** The number of reviews you can generate on these major review sites plays a significant role in your ranking performance.

- **Recent reviews.** Search engines like to see reviews that are relatively recent, ideally posted within the last six months. This demonstrates the business is active and currently worthy of high search rankings, since rankings are all about how Google views you today (and recently).

- **Average star rating.** While there is some debate as to how heavily search engines weigh average star rating, it is undoubtably one of the most important factors people judge by, so this factor should always be an important focus.

- **Review site priorities.** Google reviews are the most important for Google ranking performance, so focus first on Google reviews. It is a good idea to check out your local competitors to see how many Google reviews they have and attempt to generate at least fifty more reviews than they have. Yelp is very important on the West Coast but is less popular the farther east you go. However, Yelp reviews are sometimes syndicated into other review sites, so you can get extra benefit from good Yelp reviews. Facebook and Healthgrades are also important for both SEO and online reputation management and pretty evenly used across the country.

SOCIAL MEDIA ENGAGEMENT

In the dental industry, the two most important platforms by far are Facebook and Instagram (in that order). Social media will be discussed more extensively later on, but as social media pertains to SEO performance, the conversation is much simpler. Ideally, you should be posting content to your social media channels anywhere from two to five times every week. Simply posting content does not have much of an impact on your SEO ranking performance, but social media engagement is a big factor. If people are liking, sharing, retweeting, or commenting on your posts, this shows the search engines that you are creating engaging (valuable) content. That wins you higher SEO rankings than content that garners little to no engagement.

SERVICE RECOMMENDATION: WEO MEDIA

WEO Media is an industry leader in SEO and a certified Google Partner. They offer a transparent approach, so you will know what they're doing each month through detailed reporting, data tracking, and call tracking; documented observations; and recommendations from your SEO manager.

For more information, please see section 6, "Recommended Resources to Grow Your Practice."

PILLAR 3: PAY-PER-CLICK ADS ON GOOGLE

PPC ads are paid advertisements on Google (and other search engines) that generate traffic to your website immediately. If SEO is a marathon to getting high rankings and traffic, then PPC is more of a sprint to quick traffic generation. SEO and PPC work best when properly paired together in a coordinated fashion (ideally by the same company). These ads show up at the very top of the search results page and sometimes in the local map section or farther down the page as well.

There are a lot of misunderstandings and mistakes made regarding PPC ads on Google. These ads go by many names, including PPC, SEM (search engine marketing), Google Ads, and paid search. These are all basically the same thing—paying for clicks.

How can you target the patients you want to attract? To begin, you'll need to determine which types of patients you'd like to attract (general dentistry, orthodontics, dental implants, etc.), as well as where they're most likely to live. You can figure that out by looking at where your existing patients come from and which search terms your website already ranks high on Google for. It doesn't make sense to spend your PPC budget in areas where you're already drawing patients and ranking high on Google. The best areas in which to focus your PPC ad campaigns are the geographic areas where your patients typically come from (or could come from) but where you're not ranking high on Google.

When someone clicks on your ad, Google charges you an amount per click. Paying Google money via PPC ads has no influence or impact on your SEO rankings, as this would be completely contrary to how organic search results are determined (based on merit and user engagement, not who is paying to be there).

When a campaign is launched, it is normal to run at least two different versions of each ad, so you can test which ad is more effective (commonly known as A/B testing). Tests can analyze different ad headlines, different ad copy, different landing page layouts, different offers or calls to action, and other related items.

The actual research, design, creation, and optimization of PPC campaigns is fairly technical, so for the purposes of this book, we'll just review some high-level information you should know.

LANDING PAGE BEST PRACTICES

When people click on your PPC ad, you'll want to send them to the page of your website specifically designed for the topic of the ad. For example, if your PPC ad is about dental implants, then that click should take them to a page specifically built for dental implant leads. Many times, people do this wrong and have the link go to the home page of the website, which normally has nothing (or little) to do with the topic they clicked on. This improper landing page targeting will convert at a very low rate, whereas targeting to a well-built page on dental implants that contains educational information, videos, testimonials, and strong calls to action will convert a much higher percentage of leads.

COST PER CLICK

CPC is the amount of money the search engine charges your account each time someone clicks on your ad. When the PPC campaign is set up, your PPC manager sets a daily spending limit so you can only be charged up to a certain amount per day. Once that limit is met, your ad campaign(s) will disappear until the next day, when your budget starts all over again.

In most markets across the country, the CPC for dentistry-related terms should be under $10 per click. However, in highly competitive markets such as New York City and San Francisco, it's possible to have well-optimized CPC rates of $10–$20.

Years ago, I lectured at a study club in Texas and was explaining the concepts of PPC and CPC to the dentists in the audience. One dentist fancied himself an online marketing guru and said his PPC campaign was "really dialed in with a CPC of around $17." I had clients at that time in his same market, and we had our clients' CPC in the $4–$5 range. When I told him this, he flat out refused to believe me (by basically accusing me of lying). So I proceeded to show him a screenshot of our Google console (with the client names blacked out), which proved to him the CPC we were achieving. He was shocked. Moral of the story—hire experts who know what they are doing.

The ad budget should be set high enough so you generate enough clicks each day but not so high that you are driving up your CPC costs by going after every possible click. In most markets we recommend a starting budget between $1,000 and $2,000 per month. Once the results are looking good, you can increase the ad budget over time. Most agencies will let you adjust ad budgets with a month's notice. Your PPC manager should be able to estimate how many clicks you could generate each day (and month) in case you want to get more aggressive with your campaign(s).

QUALITY SCORE AND BOUNCE RATE

Google assigns a quality score between one and ten to each ad, with one being awful and ten being amazing. This quality score is affected by many things, including how long people stay on your page. The higher your quality score, the less Google will charge your account per click, so as your quality score improves, your CPC decreases, which allows you to generate more clicks for the same budget. The converse is also true—so if you don't know what you are doing, then Google will give you a lower quality score and charge you *more* per click. This is Google's way of encouraging you to either improve your content or advertise on a different search engine. Google wins the search engine wars by providing the best content (including ads), so if your ads are poor or your campaign is poorly run, then Google will punish you with much higher CPC costs.

A good PPC manager can usually pay for their management fee via those CPC savings because a professional PPC manager who knows what they are doing should generate a much higher quality score (and a lot more clicks for the same budget) than someone who doesn't do it all day every day

COST PER CONVERSION AND RETURN ON INVESTMENT

The most important metric from the marketing perspective on PPC campaigns is the cost per conversion. A conversion is either a phone call, appointment request, live chat lead, or direct appointment scheduling action. For example, let's say you spend $1,000 on ads for the month and generated a total of ten conversions: This would mean your cost is $100 per conversion.

However, the most important metrics to the practice are new patient acquisition cost and lead conversion rate. To close the loop in understanding a campaign's performance, you'll want to make sure you're tracking where your new patients are coming from so you can determine the campaign's return on investment (ROI). Ideally, you would get the phone call data from your PPC manager and cross-reference that with the phone numbers of new patients in your practice management software. This would help estimate cost per new patient and the ROI of the campaign. A highly complementary service to help understand all new patient calls would be to use the call analysis service by Patient Prism featured later in this section.

SERVICE RECOMMENDATION: WEO MEDIA

WEO Media is an industry leader in PPC and a certified Google Partner. They offer a transparent approach, so you will know what they are doing each month through detailed reporting, data tracking, and call tracking; documented observations; and recommendations from your PPC manager.

For more information, please see section 6, "Recommended Resources to Grow Your Practice."

PILLAR 4: ONLINE REPUTATION

In this digital age, everyone has an opinion and is clamoring to be heard, and the internet offers consumers a powerful platform on which to express themselves. Whether you have a restaurant, a law firm, or a dental practice, you can be sure that people will write reviews about you online. And while most people will have nice things to say, there will always be a few who will do their best to blast you out of business with their scathing online reviews, fairly or not.

The best way to generate more positive online reviews is to use review generation software. Many of these software platforms work in a similar fashion, using text messages and emails to ask patients to leave feedback. The best of these software platforms will integrate with your practice management software (Dentrix, Eaglesoft, Open Dental, etc.) so that the texts and emails go out automatically on the schedule you choose.

WEO Media offers an online review-generating platform called WEO Reviews. Data from the WEO Reviews platform shows that text messages have a much higher conversion rate than emails. Text messages generally convert 10 to 20 percent (or more) of the invitations into online reviews. Emails typically convert well under 5 percent. It is highly recommended that you use the software in an integrated fashion with the practice management software in order to generate a large quantity of reviews. This is far more effective than manually using the software to pick and choose who gets those review invitations.

WHAT SHOULD YOU DO ABOUT BAD REVIEWS?

Nobody likes getting a negative review about themselves or their businesses—but negative reviews will almost certainly come, so you need to be prepared to deal with them. Based on my experience working with hundreds of dental practices, there are a few best practices I like to recommend:

1. **Be proactive.** The best defense against negative reviews is a good offense. You should be consistently asking your patients to write reviews for you online. You could ask them after your appointment, send them emails with links to review sites, give them printed handouts with instructions on how to do it, or (the best option) use a software service such as WEO Reviews that automates this process with text messages and emails. If you have dozens of positive reviews, then a bad review here and there really won't matter that much, and in fact, the bad reviews can make your reviews feel more genuine since no practice is perfect.

2. **Reply to all reviews.** Review sites such as Yelp and others have published statistics that show your average star rating can actually increase when you take the time to reply to all reviews. People will see this engagement as proof that your business cares, and in some cases, reviewers will actually go back and change their rating to a higher star value. However, you must be mindful of HIPAA. Be careful not to specifically acknowledge a reviewer as a patient, and *do not* discuss anything specific about their treatment or health. Keep feedback high level, generic, and positive. It is a good idea to consult an attorney with knowledge of your state's dental rules in this area.

3. **Take the high road.** When you receive a negative review that is posted online for the world to see, it is difficult not to take it personally. Go ahead and get mad! Type out that response telling your reviewer what an idiot he is or how wrong she is—*then immediately delete it.* Get up, walk around for a few minutes, go outside to get some fresh air, and then come back to your computer in a calmer frame of mind. Now take the high road in your reply; simply say you are very sorry they had a negative experience because you place a high priority on the patient experience and putting patients first. Offer to resolve the issue by asking them to come visit the office so you can talk to them. Only respond once, and then you're done. If the reviewer responds negatively

> *Type out that response telling your reviewer what an idiot he is or how wrong she is— then immediately delete it.*

again to your comment, simply ignore it and move on. Anyone else reading the comment thread will give you the benefit of the doubt for responding positively and professionally. If you get into a back-and-forth comment battle, you won't look good, so don't do it. And again, be mindful of HIPAA as well as the communication rules in your state since each state dental board may offer different guidance on public communications.

BEWARE OF SCAMS!

Unfortunately, there are plenty of unscrupulous companies looking to profit off your negative reviews. The worst of these actually write the bad reviews themselves and then contact you to offer their "help" at getting the bad reviews removed. If you receive an email or phone call with a solicitation saying they can remove the negative reviews for a fee, you know you're dealing with a scam artist. Often the caller will state they have proprietary software that allows them to get reviews removed. This is not true; only the person who wrote the review or the review site itself can remove it. This is a common scam, so beware. If you pay them, then they will keep coming back to you to remove future bad reviews (which they will most certainly keep posting as long as you keep paying them).

SERVICE RECOMMENDATION: WEO MEDIA

WEO Media offers a highly effective online review generation/reputation management software platform called WEO Reviews.

For more information, please see section 6, "Recommended Resources to Grow Your Practice."

PILLAR 5:
SOCIAL MEDIA ENGAGEMENT

Social media accounts for a significant amount of all activity on the internet, and it is used widely across all age groups, geographies, and demographics. This makes social media an attractive way to gain exposure and new patients for your practice. The most important platforms in the dental industry are Facebook and Instagram. Note: YouTube is also critically important, but this will be covered next under pillar 6.

It is very important to set up a business page for your practice as opposed to using your personal page. Business pages have many advantages over personal pages: they list information about your practice, include clear calls to action, offer page analytics, and have the ability to advertise and offer promotions.

When setting up your business profile page, make sure you include relevant keywords that people might search for, such as your practice's name, city, and state as well as your primary service/ procedure categories (general dentistry, orthodontics, dental implants, etc.). We recommend using the following calls to action: call, email, text, and get directions.

You can engage in both free posting and paid promotional posting on both platforms.

FACEBOOK

Make it a point to encourage your existing patients to "like" your practice's Facebook page. Studies show that when people like your page, they are more likely to remain a loyal customer (patient) and are more likely to refer people to your business (practice).

Posts to your practice's Facebook page should include a combination of personalized, fun posts (60–70 percent of posts); educational oral health posts (20–30 percent of posts); and promotional/"new patient special" posts (10 percent of posts). While posting frequency is not an exact science, I recommend posting one to three times per day on the high end or two to three times per week on the low end.

Facebook offers several strategies for paid ads. You can target your ad to show up in front of friends of people who have liked your page, you can target a specific demographic, or you can do both. Ads are quite affordable on a PPC basis, so you can experiment with different headlines and offers to determine what works best.

It is recommended that you target specific subsets of your patient base, such as sedation dentistry for special needs kids or pain-free laser gum treatment for adult patients. Specific targeting tends to generate greater results. Likewise, ads that have an emotional component tend to perform better on social media than ads that are purely educational.

INSTAGRAM

Facebook and YouTube still dominate social media for most users in the United States, but Instagram has seen significant growth, especially among young adults. In 2019 Instagram, which is now owned by Facebook, reported over one billion active users worldwide, and according to the Pew Research Center, 35 percent of all US adults now use Instagram. In particular, 71 percent of adults ages 18–24 and over 50 percent of adults ages 25–29 are regular users.

According to Instagram statistics, at least 80 percent of users are now following at least one business. People want to be a part of a brand identity and to keep up with it. Advertisers in general are seeing value with Instagram ads. According to Recode.net, in the first quarter of 2017, Instagram made up 10 percent of Facebook's total ad revenue, but in the fourth quarter of 2018, it was up to about 30 percent. This is expected to continue to climb in lockstep with Instagram's growing popularity.

Instagram posting and advertising can produce a significant benefit for practices that are able to effectively engage with their patients (and potential new patients).

GROW YOUR FOLLOWER BASE

With so many businesses and users creating content, the competition for views and engagement on content is higher than ever. Here are some recommendations on what types of posts to make and how to post.

USER-GENERATED CONTENT

You don't always have to be the one to create content for your page. You can collaborate with highly engaged users (patients, friends, or colleagues) who are creating content about you. Featuring this type of content shows that a business is listening to their community and can encourage further engagement from other users. User-generated content doesn't always have to be photos and videos; it could be asking people to comment or to tag a friend, and you can feature these interactions as a post or in stories. Sometimes, encouraging engagement is as simple as asking people to pick the best emoji response to content you've posted.

For example, you can create a post asking users to share photos of their smiles using the hashtag #shareyoursmile, and this will give people a chance to be featured on your page. You can also encourage user interaction with giveaways, such as an offer to enter people in a drawing for a fun prize when they comment, share, and so on.

STORIES

Taking notes from Snapchat, Instagram and Facebook have added "stories" to their platforms, allowing users to share updates that disappear after twenty-four hours. While Facebook has not received a high amount of adoption, Instagram users frequently use the story feature to get regular updates. Stories also offer a way to create user-generated content and feedback via direct messages, polls, and submitting questions for a practice to answer. This allows for more informal, real-time updates from the practice. Ask questions, interact with followers, share news about the practice, showcase moments in your day, and have fun!

AESTHETICS

Gone are the days where you could post any photo and get decent engagement. Instagram is a highly visual platform, and though people want value beyond aesthetics, it is still important to have visually interesting, striking, or beautiful photos that draw people in to learn more and engage. Also, consistency in visuals is important for your branding. If you are posting from your mobile phone, apps such as VSCO, Snapseed, Canva, and Over are just a few of the many photo-editing apps for mobile devices.

POSTING STRATEGIES

There is a lot of conflicting information on when you should post to Instagram and how often, but in general, weekdays seem to perform best. The exact time and frequency of posts is up to you and your specific audience, but in general, think of when someone would have breaks in their day to check their phone (after waking up, during lunch, during breaks, once they get home, etc.). While it is important to post frequently to keep users engaged and keep up with Instagram's algorithm, it's also important to focus on high-value content that encourages people to interact. As for promotion we generally recommend the 90/10 rule where 90 percent is spent on teaching people new information, entertaining them, or encouraging them to interact and 10 percent can be product or service promotion. As for frequency, you could post daily if you have the bandwidth, but at least once or twice per week would be acceptable.

The majority of posts should focus on telling a story, encouraging followers to share, and providing them something that they value. Successful promotion requires trust, and trust on Instagram involves establishing yourself in a community, showing that you have a story to tell but also that you listen to and celebrate the stories of others.

As you develop your content and posting strategy for social media, you might want to consider using services that allow for the automation and prescheduling of posts. Hootsuite and Sendible are popular platforms worth exploring.

SERVICE RECOMMENDATION: WEO MEDIA

WEO Media offers a range of professional social media services for Facebook, Instagram, and other platforms. Services range from frequent, custom posting to standardized general content posting, as well as paid advertising.

For more information, please see section 6, "Recommended Resources to Grow Your Practice."

PILLAR 6: VIDEOS

One of the most underused and impactful pillars of online marketing is videos. There are many reasons to incorporate videos into your marketing:

1. Videos help improve the *website conversion* rate by educating visitors and personalizing your practice.

2. Videos help improve the *review site conversion* rate by educating visitors and personalizing your practice.

3. Videos increase *social media engagement* significantly when compared to posts without videos.

4. Videos increase *PPC ad campaign effectiveness* by educating visitors and demonstrating your expertise.

5. Videos decrease the fearful patients' anxiety about visiting the dentist by personalizing your practice, doctors, and staff.

6. Videos can get indexed and shown in search results, increasing your online exposure to potential new patients.

CUSTOM VIDEOS

Videos can be featured on your practice's website, on social media platforms, on review sites, and in the waiting room. There are several primary categories of videos to incorporate into your practice's marketing, including

- practice overview videos,

- patient testimonial videos, and

- FAQ videos.

Videos typically feature a combination of A-roll and B-roll footage. A-roll is footage of a person speaking directly into the camera, whereas B-roll includes background footage such as the outside of the building, the waiting room, the operatories, equipment and technology, and people interacting.

PRACTICE OVERVIEW VIDEOS

A practice overview video incorporates A-roll and B-roll to develop a narrative about your practice. The goal is to convince patients to visit your practice by educating viewers about your practice's personality, doctors, staff, equipment, and expertise. These videos should be shot by professional videographers and be about one to two minutes in length. Practice overview videos should be placed on the home page of the practice's website, ideally in the top half of the website. It is highly recommended that you use a professional videographer for your practice overview video.

PATIENT TESTIMONIAL VIDEOS

Patient testimonial videos are highly impactful at connecting with potential patients, especially when the patient and the person on the video have commonalities such as age, gender, life stage, or concern about going to the dentist.

These videos can be located on the home page of the website as well as on a dedicated patient testimonials page and should be between thirty seconds and two minutes long. Ideally, these videos would be professionally produced, but you can shoot these yourself. To do this you'll need a quiet space that is well lit. You'll want to purchase a tripod, a digital camera that can rest on the tripod, and a lavalier microphone to connect to the digital camera. A little practice is all that is needed to set up your own video production studio. If you're not sure how to do this, just search on YouTube, and there will be plenty of videos that show you how to do it.

FAQ VIDEOS

Patients often have questions, so it can be a powerful tactic to create a series of videos that answer the most commonly asked questions you hear in your practice. These videos can be featured on an FAQ page on your website as well as web pages on that specific topic. For example, you may produce a video about dental implants that discusses the overall philosophy, implant technology you use, equipment you use, and any related topic you think would be of interest to patients. A service-based video like that can be placed on the website's FAQ page as well as a dental implant page. These types of videos are also very helpful for SEO rankings when people are searching for a specific question such as "How much does a dental implant cost?" or any number of similar searches. Think about the most common questions you get from your patients, and create a video for each question.

All three of these video types can be effective when posted on social media channels and review sites.

MARKETING RELEASE FORM

In this section there have been many ideas and concepts presented, some of which involve patients. It is highly recommended that you ask your patients to sign a marketing release form that allows you to use their images, videos, comments, and so on in your practice's marketing. I always advise practices to consult with their state dental boards and an attorney who is familiar with the relevant requirements to remain legally compliant and HIPAA compliant when they're developing their forms.

VIDEO HOSTING

If you decide to develop your own videos, I usually advise hosting them on YouTube since it is easy to use, and YouTube videos are indexed in Google search results, so there is an opportunity to gain significant SEO benefit.

SERVICE RECOMMENDATION: WEO MEDIA

WEO Media has produced hundreds of professional videos all over North America. Their team of dental video experts can produce a wide range of videos on site at your practice including practice overview videos, patient testimonial videos, and FAQ videos.

For more information, please see section 6, "Recommended Resources to Grow Your Practice."

PATIENT EDUCATION VIDEOS

The most highly visited pages on dental websites are the home page and doctor bio/team pages, followed by the service pages on topics such as cosmetic dental services, restorative procedures, specialty procedures, and so on. The best way to improve the engagement and patient education benefit on these pages is to embed educational videos on each dental service page. These videos help convert more leads on the website and can be used by clinicians to increase case acceptance rate.

DEAR DOCTOR

Dear Doctor provides video products designed to educate the dental patient. Their variety of products all serve to promote dentistry in a positive light and educate patients in a way that leads to positive oral health decisions, resulting in greater follow-through in scheduling appointments, increased inquiries about services, and ultimately greater case acceptance. Their primary services include a website video library, Dear Doctor TV, and Consult Assistant.

WEBSITE VIDEO LIBRARY

Dear Doctor website videos are designed for the patient who is exploring various dental services and procedures. Patients can find clear information presented by a reassuring host in easy-to-understand language supplemented by animations and illustrations designed to be informative without gory details that might put off a patient. Their videos explain the benefits of treatment and encourage patients to see the dentist, making them more likely to schedule an appointment. The risks of not seeing a dentist are conveyed in a direct but not intimidating way so patients will understand the importance of seeing the dentist to address oral health problems early.

DEAR DOCTOR TV

Dear Doctor TV helps educate patients who are in the waiting room and those throughout the practice. Informational treatment videos are interspersed with dental-themed entertainment, trivia, and celebrity interviews. In addition, dentists can easily add their own practice-specific content to the broadcast.

CONSULT ASSISTANT

Dear Doctor Consult Assistant is a chairside educational tool that can be used on a tablet, PC, or television (through the Dear Doctor TV platform). This product is intended for the patient who is in the dental office for a particular treatment. It has intuitive navigation and videos designed specifically for chairside use. The dentist or staff can select specific videos to help improve case acceptance and better prepare the patient for treatment.

For more information, please see section 6, "Recommended Resources to Grow Your Practice."

DIRECT-TO-CONSUMER MARKETING

Once your online marketing is robust and dialed in, it's time to consider D2C marketing campaigns. The most popular D2C option in the dental industry by far is direct mail campaigns. There are many vendors available to provide this service, so the most important factors you'll want to evaluate are their experience in dental campaigns, typical case study results, results tracking, and pricing/ROI. Campaigns can target based on geographic area or more specifically with demographic targeting. It is also wise to include an attractive offer and/or call to action to increase the response rate.

In terms of tracking results, you'll want to use a dedicated tracking phone number for each campaign in order to measure leads generated and ROI. It is important to understand that the tracking phone number will not capture all the leads generated since many people will go to the website (and/or other online properties). This is why it is important to first understand your baseline website performance so you can more accurately estimate the additional traffic and phone calls coming from your direct mail campaign. Even more important is to have your office staff consistently ask, "How did you hear about us?" and enter that information into your practice management software. This will be explored in more detail in section 4.

In addition to direct mail, other D2C techniques that can be effective are radio ads, print ads, and TV ads. For D2C campaigns you'll want to research the targeting for the ads to make sure they are in both the proper geographic area and demographics you're targeting. Be sure to use unique phone numbers to track each D2C campaign so you know just where your results are coming from.

STEP 2: CONVERTING LEADS INTO APPOINTMENTS

Now that we've covered how to generate leads, let's convert those leads into appointments! Based on data analysis of hundreds of dental practices, I've found the typical percentage of patient leads will contact the practice as follows:

- Phone calls = 85–99 percent

- 24/7 live chat = 0–5 percent

- Online appointment scheduling = 0–5 percent

- Appointment request form submission = 0–3 percent

PHONE CALLS

By far the largest conversion option is phone calls. The use of tracking phone numbers is critical to help measure and understand the performance of marketing campaigns. *If you don't use a tracking number on your website, then your online marketing is flying blind.*

There are two primary approaches to answering the phone: (1) answer the phone yourself or (2) outsource to a call center.

ANSWERING CALLS IN HOUSE

If your staff is tasked with answering the phones in house, there are two great services that come highly recommended to improve the conversion rate: Patient Prism and Weave.

PATIENT PRISM

Patient Prism is a best-of-class, award-winning solution to one of the biggest problems in dentistry: getting people to book an appointment. While other call tracking companies tell you how potential patients found your dental practice, Patient Prism quickly provides call analysis and training your team needs to convert more callers into booked appointments.

Patient Prism tracks, records, and provides coaching on new patient phone calls using a combination of artificial intelligence, machine learning, and experienced dental call coaches. Every time a potential patient ends the phone call without booking an appointment, Patient Prism sends an alert to the dental practice typically within an hour, detailing what the caller wanted, why the caller didn't book, and effective phrasing the team can use to quickly call back the patient and convert that lost opportunity into a booked appointment. The alert even includes short, one-minute videos of dental industry leaders demonstrating exactly what to say. Wise practices will assign a person to follow up on these new patient leads as they come in since data from Patient Prism shows this can really improve new patient flow.

Best of all, the front desk team doesn't need to listen to the recorded phone calls. Who has time? Patient Prism's patented solution displays the information in a visual format so it takes only a few seconds to understand what happened on that new patient call.

Wouldn't it be nice to know what you should say when a caller asks about insurance, costs, scheduling, or any of the other reasons that frequently prevent people from booking an appointment? Patient Prism provides answers for hundreds of situations.

For more information, please see section 6, "Recommended Resources to Grow Your Practice."

WEAVE

Weave offers a phone solution integrated with patient communication tools such as appointment reminders, essentially providing personalized communication in an automated fashion. There are several really cool features in particular: a screen pop feature, missed call text messaging, and a powerful app.

When a patient calls the practice, detailed patient information pops up on the screen before the phone is even picked up. This allows the office to treat the patient like a friend, rather than asking twenty questions to verify their information. This is a powerful way to strengthen patient-practice relations.

Most potential new patients who call a practice, if they are sent to voicemail, will hang up and call the next practice on their Google search page. Weave will automatically send a personalized, customized text within five seconds of them hanging up, stating something like "This is Sara with Dr. Smith's office. I am currently assisting another patient but will call you back in three to five minutes. You can also text me back here if you prefer. Speak with you shortly." This really impresses patients and prevents numerous lost opportunities to acquire new patients.

The Weave app allows the doctor or team to pull up the schedule on their phone and make calls or send texts from their mobile device with the patients seeing such communications as coming from the practice's number.

Overall, the Weave service offering will significantly reduce cancellations and missed calls while also increasing appointments from both new and existing patients.

Both of these services are highly effective, affordable tools to greatly improve the call performance of your staff. My recommendation is to use both!

For more information, please see section 6, "Recommended Resources to Grow Your Practice."

CALL CENTER OUTSOURCING

If you decide your practice would be better off outsourcing some (or all) of your incoming and outgoing calls, then a call center can be a great option to consider.

Call centers offer several advantages over answering the phone yourself. They can answer the phone 24/7, all year long. This can typically be structured in a variety of ways. For example, the call center can answer all incoming calls or only new patient calls. They can answer calls after a set number of rings or only during certain hours of the day and days of the week. Overall, call centers offer maximum flexibility to make sure you don't miss those valuable incoming calls.

Another significant benefit is surge capacity. It is quite common during certain times of the day to receive multiple calls at the same time. Since call centers typically have dozens of operators, they usually have the ability to answer all incoming calls at all times.

In addition, call operators do the same thing all day long—answer calls from dental patients. This specialization allows them to perform much better at converting calls into appointments than most practice staff.

Most call centers offer outbound calling as well, although this is usually a small percentage of their overall call load. Outbound calling can be beneficial to quickly follow up on missed new patient opportunities.

Even if you outsource to a call center I would still recommend using Patient Prism so you can see how they are doing and give them tools to do a better job for your practice.

24/7 LIVE CHAT

Offering 24/7 live chat on a website is a great way to engage with patients in real time, especially after hours, when the practice is not typically answering the phone. Regardless of the time of day or day of the week, there will always be a small percentage of people who would rather engage in live chat than call the office directly. For these people live chat is a great way for the office to engage in a conversation and hopefully schedule an appointment.

Even if a practice is answering 100 percent of their calls, they will still benefit from 24/7 live chat since some people would rather chat than call. The idea is to capture as many new patient leads as possible, so this tool is one every practice should use.

While there are a variety of 24/7 chat tools on the market, most either need to be staffed by your employees or by a third party who will only be able to engage in conversations to collect information. The best 24/7 live chat option allows the chat operator to schedule appointments directly into the practice management software, which takes new patient lead conversion to the next level.

Practices with high website traffic will naturally experience the most new patient conversions, so it is recommended that you invest in SEO and PPC in order to get maximum benefit from your live chat service.

SERVICE RECOMMENDATION: AMPLIFY BY SIMPLIFEYE

Simplifeye offers a 24/7 live chat service called Amplify, which is staffed by dental professionals. Amplify has the ability to schedule appointments directly into your practice management software and can be added to any website.

For more information, please see section 6, "Recommended Resources to Grow Your Practice."

ONLINE APPOINTMENT SCHEDULING

There are third-party, online appointment scheduling software tools that can be linked from the website, allowing a patient to identify the specific day and time they wish to visit their desired location. Some tools allow the patient to actually schedule into the practice management software, whereas other tools are basically a fancy appointment request form. Also, some practice management software systems offer a patient scheduling portal you can link to from the website. It is a good idea to identify which option would work best for your practice and link to it from your website.

WEBSITE APPOINTMENT REQUEST FORM

Every website should at a minimum have an appointment request form. However, if the website already has online appointment scheduling software integration, then you probably don't need to also include this form, as it would be redundant and possibly confusing to patients. The priority would be to have an appointment scheduling option, but a backup plan would be a simple appointment request form.

STEP 3: CONVERT APPOINTMENTS INTO SOLD DENTISTRY (CASE ACCEPTANCE)

Now that we've generated new patient leads and scheduled their appointments, we're well on our way to practice growth. The last step in this new patient generation process is to have these patients accept treatment in the office (a.k.a. case acceptance). There are many ways to approach the optimization of case acceptance. In particular, staff training is the most important, but there are several noteworthy tools and services that can also help.

STAFF TRAINING: UNDERSTANDING A PATIENT'S CORE VALUES

Case acceptance is truly one of the most important factors to focus on for practice growth, yet so many practices don't make it a priority to track and improve.

The coaches at Fortune Management are experts at increasing case acceptance and offer this advice for doctors and staff alike:

When considering making a purchase, the perceived value of an item or service needs to be greater than the cost or people are not likely to buy. When it comes to dentistry, patients need to have a clear understanding of what's happening in their mouths. If there is no discomfort, patients often don't feel they have a problem that needs to be solved; therefore they don't value the diagnosis.

Asking questions that confirm patients understand their oral problems, the clinical solutions, and consequences of inaction will help your team determine whether patients truly understand the value of treatment.

All patients have a core value, which is what matters most to them apart from the clinical aspects of dentistry. To find out a patient's core value, you simply need to ask:

"Mrs. Smith, what's most important to you about your oral health and the dental care you would like to receive?"

"Well, I'm pretty busy; I work and I have three kids. So I don't have a lot of time for dental visits."

This question and the subsequent answer will help the team identify the patient's core values, which typically are related to five specific things: money, time/convenience, quality, comfort, or relationships. The next question identifies the rules this specific patient has for that core value.

A follow-up question would be "I understand that time is extremely valuable to you. Would you mind sharing with me what has to happen in order for you to feel we have valued your time?"

This patient might reply by saying, "I would love to be seen on time and, if possible, to have all my care done in as few visits as possible." Once you have identified the patient's core values and their rules, you can then identify what your practice can offer that aligns with the patient's most important wants. In Mrs. Smith's case, it is time. So when you present recommended treatment, you would explain the clinical and health value of the dentistry but also detail how the technology you have in your practice will enable Mrs. Smith to enjoy one-day crowns, minimizing her time investment at the practice.

"Mrs. Smith, as you know, I'm recommending we put crowns on two of your teeth that have cracks. I've showed you on the monitor how serious this issue is and shared with you my concerns that if you don't take care of this now, one or both may break and not only cause discomfort but additional expense. You indicated you want to get this taken care of but also mentioned time is very valuable to you. The good news is we have technology that will enable us to do your crowns in just one visit so we don't interrupt your work schedule or take too much time away from your family."

Dentists and their teams have to make sure the patient knows that you care about them and that you really care about getting them healthy.

GETTING PATIENTS TO **YES**—SHOW THEM YOU CARE

We've all heard the saying, "People don't care how much you know until they know how much you care." This is especially true in dentistry. Dentists and their teams have to make sure the patient knows that you care about them and that you really care about getting them healthy. In addition to delivering an exceptional experience that centers around the patient and providing value, here are a few ways you can let patients know your goal is to care for them, not treat them.

Always use the word *care* instead of *treatment*. (Please forgive me for not taking my own advice and using *treatment* throughout the book since this book is not intended for patients.)

Always make care as easy as possible. This may mean being available for appointments beyond traditional work hours and keeping a small number of empty slots in your schedule for same-day appointments. You may want to evaluate staying open late or opening early one day a week. Likewise, you may want to consider weekend appointments (if your staff is on board).

Always follow up with patients after their appointments to see how they're doing. You can do this with a phone call or personal note mailed to them. (Note: This can be a good time to ask for an online review on Google, Facebook, Yelp, or Healthgrades.)

Always keep great notes in the patient's file. Know who their family is and key dates and important events in their lives. Using a service such as Weave can help personalize these types of patient communications.

Always show appreciation. A simple "Thank you for choosing our practice as your dental home" can go a long way. This could be done verbally, via email, or better yet with a handwritten note mailed to them.

INTRAORAL CAMERAS

Using visual aids that enable patients to literally "see" the issues with their teeth can be very beneficial. Intraoral cameras have become the industry standard to show patients potential and existing problems in their mouth. In fact, I have personally experienced the power of intraoral cameras with case acceptance.

For years I had visited the same dentist, and he would occasionally mention that my amalgam fillings were wearing out and I should probably have them replaced soon. He didn't really convey a sense of urgency and didn't show me what was going on. This went on for several years. He eventually moved, so I had to find a new dentist. During my first visit at the new practice, I immediately noticed the nice, modern layout and use of technology throughout the office. After my exam and X-rays, the dentist showed me some pictures of my teeth from the intraoral camera his assistant had just used during my exam. When he showed me pictures of my amalgam fillings, pointing out where they were worn on the edges and decay could start spreading, that was all I needed to see. I scheduled an appointment to have my fillings replaced, and I can say I'm really glad I did.

The only differences between my treatment denial and acceptance was the sense of urgency and use of intraoral camera pictures. The fact that the dentist took the time to explain what was going on and what would eventually happen was helpful, but what sealed the deal were those pictures of my fillings. Yuck! Sometimes clinicians forget how powerful pictures can be to the nondental professional. If you are not using intraoral cameras, then you should start using them as soon as possible in order to improve your case acceptance.

AFFORDABILITY AND FINANCING OPTIONS

In an ideal world, price wouldn't matter to patients who need dental treatment, but in the real world, price matters—a lot! Fortunately, there are some nice options available to help patients pay for the dentistry they want and need.

The leader in the patient financing space is CareCredit. For over thirty years, CareCredit has been providing a valuable financing option for treatments and procedures that typically are not covered by insurance or for times when insurance doesn't cover the full amount. CareCredit is also used by cardholders to pay for deductibles and copayments.

In general, people like having financial options because it gives them the freedom to make decisions about treatment options. This allows them to do what's best for their situation and their family. Your clinical staff should all become well versed about patient financing options.

SERVICE RECOMMENDATION: CARECREDIT

CareCredit provides a valuable financing option for treatments and procedures that typically are not covered by insurance or for times when insurance doesn't cover the full amount. CareCredit is also used by cardholders to pay for deductibles and copayments.

For more information, please see section 6, "Recommended Resources to Grow Your Practice."

PATIENT LOYALTY PROGRAMS

Patient loyalty/membership programs are growing in popularity and provide practices with an additional way to overcome objections to treatment acceptance. Membership plans improve access to oral care and provide the simplicity, ease of use, and price transparency patients desire.

Membership plans have been shown to improve patient loyalty and frequency of visits, which contribute to improved oral health. Likewise, membership plans can increase practice production and profitability through higher case acceptance and recall rates. An additional benefit of membership plans is that they allow dental practices to take some control back from insurance companies.

Patients using membership plans are highly desirable because they normally accept a higher percentage of treatment than uninsured patients and are typically quite a bit more profitable than insured patients. However, success will be fleeting without high member renewal rates, so make sure your membership program addresses retention.

While there are quite a few options for membership plans on the market, Kleer is particularly impressive. For patients, Kleer membership plans provide a simple, comprehensive, and affordable dental care plan that enables them to take a proactive approach to manage their oral health. Better yet, Kleer is free for practices to implement.

SERVICE RECOMMENDATION: KLEER

Kleer is an advanced, cloud-based platform that enables a dental practice to easily design and manage their own membership plan and offer it directly to their uninsured patients. Kleer is turnkey and *free* to implement and includes everything a practice needs to create and manage a successful membership plan.

For more information, please see section 6, "Recommended Resources to Grow Your Practice."

MARKETING FOR SPECIFIC SERVICES

O
ne of the great benefits of marketing is the ability to target messaging for specific services in specific geographies. This is a fantastic way to increase new patient flow, especially for services the practice would prefer to be doing (e.g., those that are more profitable, more enjoyable, etc.).

Most practices I've worked with to develop marketing programs have specific services they wish to preferentially target. The most popular of these are dental implants, orthodontics, cosmetic dentistry, and sleep dentistry.

The online marketing approach is very similar for all these services, so for the purpose of illustration, we'll focus this section on dental implant marketing. Keep in mind this approach reflects essentially the same methodology for the other services as well.

DENTAL IMPLANT MARKETING

Since 2014 I've been fortunate to work closely with one of the premier dental implant companies in the world and have developed deep expertise in the area of dental implant marketing. Nobel Biocare is a worldwide market leader in offering solutions from root to tooth, covering dental implants; restorative components; individualized, patient-specific prosthetics; and biomaterials. Additionally, Nobel Biocare runs a training and education program for dental professionals across the globe.

There are many aspects to developing a dental implant marketing program. The first thing to consider is the type of practice: referral driven or marketing driven. Most dental specialists who place implants are referral driven, at least as their primary form of growth. This group includes oral and maxillofacial surgeons, periodontists, prosthodontists, and in some cases endodontists. They often rely on general dentists to refer most of their patients to them. For this group the prospect of aggressive marketing for new patients runs the risk of alienating some of their referring general dentists since their marketing could be viewed as competing for the same patients.

The good news for referral-driven specialist practices is that a solid online marketing program can achieve the best of both worlds. Online marketing is much more under the radar than D2C marketing, so a dental specialist can effectively (and even aggressively) market for new patients online without much risk of straining referral relationships with general dentists. Therefore, both referral-driven and marketing-driven practices can benefit from online marketing targeting specific services such as dental implants.

KEY MARKETING PROGRAM ELEMENTS

As you begin to market for patients willing to pay for premium services such as dental implants, it is important to realize that simply providing some basic information on your website is not enough.

When considering which doctor to select for providing their dental implants, patients are willing to do far more research than just picking a general dentist for normal preventive dentistry. As a general rule, the more expensive the procedure, the more research a patient will do.

As a general rule, the more expensive the procedure, the more research a patient will do.

WEBSITE ELEMENTS

The practice's website should contain testimonials from successful dental implant patients as well as before and after photos. The most powerful type of testimonials are video testimonials in which the emotional impact of getting needed treatment can be better communicated to potential patients watching the videos. Dental implants can be life changing for the patient, allowing them to smile with confidence, go out in public on dates, socialize with friends, and eat foods they may not have been able to enjoy in years. Capturing this type of life-changing impact will make a significant impression on a potential patient considering your practice.

In addition to patient testimonial videos, the practice's website (and YouTube channel) should contain a practice overview video on the website's home page. This video should highlight all the reasons to choose your practice as their dental implant provider, including items such as the use of premium quality dental implants (such as implants from Nobel Biocare), CBCT (cone-beam computed tomography) technology, education level, training experience (e.g., continuing education [CE] courses and implant programs), procedural experience (e.g., hundreds or thousands of implants placed), and any other related factors. Likewise, if you are using any sort of new, cutting-edge technology such as an X-Guide (3-D–guided implant surgery), then this should be featured prominently in order to further differentiate you as a leader in your local or regional market.

Patient education videos specifically about dental implants are also highly recommended. These videos could be stock videos (e.g., from Dear Doctor), be provided by the supplier (e.g., Nobel Biocare), or be professionally produced featuring the actual doctor(s) discussing their philosophy, technology, experience, and techniques.

ONLINE REPUTATION

The online reputation of the practice should be stellar. The target would be to have at least a 4.0-star average rating on the major review sites including Google, Yelp, Facebook, and Healthgrades (although a 4.5-star rating or above is really the level to target). Any practice with star rating averages under 4.0 should first focus on improving these levels before engaging in expensive and aggressive marketing campaigns.

LEAD GENERATION

Marketing to generate leads for dental implants can target a larger demographic area than normal new patient marketing. The reason for this is the more expensive the procedure, the farther patients are willing to travel for the dentist they determine to be the best fit for them. This is similar to buying a car in terms of the amount of research and willingness to travel involved.

Therefore, PPC ad campaigns are normally a large percentage of the overall marketing budget since PPC allows for much broader geographic coverage than any other form of online marketing. For dental implants in particular, I have found Google PPC to be the most effective (as compared to Facebook or social media in general).

If you max out the available Google PPC budget for your target area, then the second priority should be Bing PPC ads, and the third priority would be Facebook PPC ads.

This is not to say that SEO is not important—quite the opposite, in fact. You'll want to work with your SEO agency to make sure you rank as highly as possible for as many geographies as possible. Just keep in mind that it is often difficult to rank in an organic (nonpaid) Google search for geographies where you don't have a physical office address. This is why Google PPC ads end up being the majority of an online marketing program targeting dental implants.

SEM is another consideration, although generally not near the top of my list. This approach allows for banner ads and retargeting processes, which use cookies to track people who have clicked on your ads and then follow them around the internet, popping your ad up on various websites they visit. This technique is widely used in e-commerce for product sales, but I have not found it to be an effective marketing strategy for dental services.

D2C MARKETING CONSIDERATIONS

For general dentists and dental specialists who are not too concerned with more overt and obvious forms of marketing, there are several viable options to consider.

DIRECT MAIL

Direct mail campaigns are by far the most popular form of D2C marketing in the dental industry. When designing a direct mail ad campaign, you'll want to make sure you are incorporating a compelling offer to improve ad response rates. This usually involves something such as a set amount of dollars off the procedure or a free consultation, exam, and X-ray.

It is really important to use a dedicated (unique) call-tracking phone number so you can attempt to track calls generated from the campaign(s). The mailers should include this unique tracking phone number as well as a dedicated (unique) landing page for people to visit.

There are pros and cons to directing people to a unique landing page as opposed to the main website. Unique landing pages can increase tracking accuracy since it is more difficult to track direct mail responses once they are on the main practice website. However, the downside to a landing page is the fact that the conversion rate may suffer. For practices with sufficient budgets, I recommend doing both—have one direct mail campaign that goes to a dedicated landing page and one that goes to the main website. If there is a measurable difference in response rate, then you can focus on the campaign type that works best for your practice.

In addition, it is common to implement A/B testing on direct marketing campaigns where you would run two different versions of an ad in the same market at the same time. As you measure response rate, the more effective ads will be determined, and you can continue to test and optimize as you go. Common items to vary during A/B testing are the mailer messaging, mailer offer, landing page layout, and landing page calls to action.

RADIO, PRINT, AND TV

These forms of D2C marketing are generally more expensive than direct mail campaigns and also tend to be more unpredictable. There are large national chains that spend millions of dollars to market for dental implant patients using radio, print, and TV ads. However, for most practices this large-scale approach is not feasible due to the costs involved.

If you decide to pursue radio, print, or TV, I would prioritize them in this order: (1) radio, (2) print, and (3) TV. Radio campaigns can be effective on both AM and FM, but it really comes down to proper demographic targeting. You'll want to work with the radio station to explain your target market and let them show you the best options to fit your situation.

The more office locations you have in a geographic marketing area, the more likely D2C campaigns will work well for you.

Print ads include newspapers, magazines, journals and inserts for publications. Print ads can be effective, but they are usually break-even endeavors in my experience.

TV ads can be highly effective, but more often than not they tend to lose money.

There are other forms of direct marketing you may want to experiment with such as billboards, movie theater screen ads (appearing before the movie starts), and local/regional magazines.

A major factor in the effectiveness of D2C marketing campaigns is your geographic coverage. The more office locations you have in a geographic marketing area, the more likely D2C campaigns will work well for you. However, if you only have a few locations, then I highly recommend sticking with online marketing until you have at least five or more locations in a marketing region (meaning one campaign would cover at least five offices in the media coverage area of the ad).

YOUR SECRET WEAPON:
THE DENTAL IMPLANT COMPANY

Believe it or not, the dental implant company you choose can have a major impact on the success of your dental implant marketing programs. While marketing is the start of the process, it is even more important to have the right team in place to execute clinically and operationally.

WEO Media has worked with hundreds of practices that market for dental implants. The vast majority of our clients who are doing large volumes of implant patients are those practices that use a premium implant supplier such as Nobel Biocare.

There are many reasons for this correlation between implant volume and implant provider. Low-cost implant providers simply sell titanium screws and components and provide very little service, support, or business development assistance.

Contrast that with the numerous benefits I have witnessed Nobel Biocare provide their doctor customers:

- **Business strategy support.** The Nobel Biocare sales team works with their doctors to identify areas for growth and improved partnering with the practice to develop an annual practice development plan. This is essentially like having your own business development support team with tons of experience in generating implant patients and growing implant sales. Low-cost providers do not offer this type of critical business support.

- **Training and personal development.** Nobel provides its clinicians with unparalleled access to thought leaders and experts by bringing them to your practice for CE events and study clubs. Nobel Biocare also offers in-depth CE training on the latest products, solutions, and technologies at their world-class training facilities as well as via webinar. Additionally, Nobel Biocare partners with numerous implant training programs to help meet your training needs at competitive prices.

- **Practice growth tools.** To enable doctors to grow their practices, Nobel provides a curated set of tools—from patient education TV (NobelVision) and digital media services to referral management, office management, and CE credits. Read more about these tools at www.nobelbiocare.com/practicegrowth.

- **Dedicated customer service.** With Nobel Biocare, you are provided support every step of the way from their team of knowledgeable customer service representatives.

- **Lifetime warranty.** Nobel Biocare's product and treatment concepts are designed to give patients fully functional and natural-looking restorations that aspire to last a lifetime. Nobel Biocare offers a lifetime warranty for many of their products. Doctors should inquire directly with Nobel Biocare for specific details.

- **Brand recognition and credibility.** Nobel Biocare is perhaps the most recognized dental implant brand on the planet and is well known to be a high-quality, premium implant provider. Nobel invests millions of dollars in research and development to stay at the leading edge of dental implant technology. There are only a few companies in the world that come close to this type of investment and commitment. This is a big marketing advantage when educating potential patients as to why they should choose your practice over other practices using cheaper and lower-quality products.

CASE ACCEPTANCE

Once you've dialed in your marketing campaigns and are up and running with support from your premium implant provider, a critical aspect of your implant marketing program's success lies in case acceptance.

In addition to the case acceptance tips presented earlier, it can be well worth the investment to get training from experts who specialize in dental implant case acceptance. Nobel Biocare has a group of experts and consultants they can mobilize to help your practice in this area. If you are serious about dental implant marketing, then it is critical to focus on developing your staff in this area.

For more information about Nobel Biocare, please see section 6, "Recommended Resources to Grow Your Practice."

TRACKING RESULTS

"Should I be spending more
on SEO and PPC?"

"How can I tell what advertising
is working and what isn't?"

"I've been burned by three other marketing
companies. How are you guys any different?"

hear questions such as these all too often, and they tell you a
lot about what's wrong with our industry. Marketing companies
ostensibly in business to help their dentist clients market their
practices often sell them a laundry list of services and products on
the premise they'll help them attract the new patients they need—
but then the companies fail to deliver. Thus, the doctors find themselves paying for results that never materialize or end up in the dark
regarding what did work versus what didn't. That leads to frustration
and an understandable mistrust of marketers in general.

The biggest issue? I believe it's a lack of transparency coupled
with a lack of accountability. If you as the client don't really know
where the money's going or what the actual, quantifiable results are,

you're in the dark—and you shouldn't be. Doctors tend to be lifelong learners and comfortable with digesting data-driven concepts. Marketing is part art and part science and is growing increasingly more precise. It's important that you understand the moving parts that make up a marketing effort and how to track each part of the effort. If you don't understand exactly what's working (or failing) to bring in new patients to your practice, or why some kinds of advertising spend work better than others, you need a marketer who will help you understand that and the tools to make it easy for you to keep up with the incoming data tracking your results.

When you're conducting a marketing program or any kind of program intended to bring new patients into your practice, it is critical to understand just where those patients came from. That's why every dental practice should be using their practice management software (PMS) as a method of tracking their results in addition to its uses as a scheduling tool and for storing patient information.

Every time a new patient comes in, whoever is checking them in at the front office should ask, "How did you hear about us?" and make sure that that information is accurately entered into the PMS, with the proper coding as to referral source. Then at the end of each month, you can download a new patient report to analyze where all your new patients are coming from. Typically, you should be tracking your new patient counts, how they came to the practice, what your marketing spend has been and then use that information to calculate (or approximate) your ROI. These KPIs show you how you're doing, providing a sort of business dashboard that lets you accurately assess what's working and what isn't.

TRACKING YOUR MARKETING

There are multiple ways in which you can track where your leads are coming from. One method is to use tracking phone numbers: in particular one number for your website and online properties and one number for your Google PPC ads. That lets you see how many calls are coming from your organic website traffic versus the calls being generated via paid ads and paid searches. Please remember to use one tracking phone number for all your online properties or you risk a penalty from Google and other search engines. When search engines see different contact information (name, address, and phone number) displayed across different online properties, they assume something is wrong. They don't know which piece of information is wrong, and as a result they greatly reduce your search rankings (SEO performance) due to their lack of confidence in your discrepant information. Google makes a special exception for PPC ads if you use the code they provide. This allows for a tracking number to be used on PPC ads without hurting your SEO performance.

However, if you're also doing offline D2C advertising, such as direct mail, billboards, radio, television, or print ads, each of those campaigns should also get its own tracking number. That helps you determine which of these marketing initiatives is generating calls and which aren't as effective. You'll need to keep in mind that many leads generated from D2C marketing will go online before contacting the office, so your tracked calls associated with D2C marketing will almost always be understated and online marketing results overstated. Again, this is why your office staff must consistently ask new patients, "How did you hear about us?" At the end of the month, your marketing coordinator can review and summarize the results using your PMS and business analytic software to approximate as closely as possible what's working and what's not.

One client I worked with had over ninety active tracking numbers because they had a large marketing budget. Without accurate tracking they would have wasted a lot of money on campaigns that performed poorly. Not only did we track all these individual numbers but we also tracked and reported how effective each office was at properly filling out the "How did you hear about us?" field in the PMS. This focus really helped improve tracking compliance, which resulted in better data, analysis, and ROI.

ESTABLISH A BASELINE

As you work to understand your marketing performance, it's really important to establish a baseline with your website traffic and generated calls. Once your online marketing is fairly well optimized, you should settle into a range for website traffic and generated calls. You may know, for instance, that you're getting between 500 and 600 visitors a month to your website and 80 to 120 calls per month. Then you run a radio ad, and suddenly that number spikes to 800 visitors and 150 calls the following month. You could reasonably deduce that a good chunk (or perhaps all) of this increase came from the radio ad. However, if you haven't yet established your baselines, then it is more difficult to be certain what's actually prompting those calls. That's why establishing baselines with your online marketing should come first, ahead of D2C marketing. This serves as a nice reality check on your PMS's new patient tracking data.

Tracking results can get confusing if you have multiple D2C campaigns running simultaneously. Your website traffic is likely to be jumping all over the place, and it becomes more challenging to discern just which of these campaigns is causing the increases on the website. Some people decide to get aggressive with their marketing, effectively using a scattershot approach—and that's fine as long as you understand that the trade-off is you'll have less ability to track the one-to-one correlation of a specific marketing initiative to your results. The flip side to this coin is that if your office staff is really good at asking "How did you hear about us?" and putting that into your PMS, then running multiple marketing campaigns at the same time is less of a tracking issue to decipher.

DETERMINING RETURN ON INVESTMENT

The best way to understand how economically effective your specific marketing efforts are is to start with a high-level view of your total marketing spend and your total new patient generation. Divide your total marketing spend by the number of new patients you've gotten in that time period, and calculate what the patient acquisition cost has been. This will provide a top-level summary. For an example, see the table below.

	April	May	June
New patients	30	25	30
Total marketing spend	$4,000	$4,000	$4,000
Acquisition cost per patient	$133	$160	$133

The next step will be to dive deeper by looking at each major marketing category (SEO, PPC, social media, direct mail, etc.) and listing the marketing spend for each category. Now here is where the accuracy of your new patient tracking becomes critical. You should summarize where every new patient came from and assign these patients to the appropriate marketing category.

Most practices will also have a significant number of new patients who did not come from marketing but from other sources such as patient referrals, employee referrals, PPO insurance websites, walk-ins, and so on. You should assign new patients by category as accurately as possible, match that with the marketing spend or cost for that category, and calculate your estimated ROI for each category.

Month: April	New Patients	Marketing Spend	Patient Acquisition Cost
SEO	10	$1,000	$100
PPC	7	$2,250	$321
Social media	3	$500	$167
Insurance referrals*	2	-	-
Walk-ins	3	-	-
Referrals	5	$250	$50
Total	30	$4,000	$133

*Note: While insurance referrals did not directly incur a marketing cost, it would be a good idea to look at the fee discounts to determine if insurance patients are profitable. This is not the traditional patient acquisition cost calculation but more of a profitability analysis of your various insurance providers.

This exercise will shed light on to what is really driving your new patient growth. Once you know what is working well, you may decide to spend more budget on those areas and reduce the budget in underperforming areas.

UNDERSTANDING PATIENT ECONOMIC VALUE

Typically, a patient is worth around $800–$1,000 a year to a general dentistry practice, so if you can acquire a new patient for between $100 and $200, you're getting a pretty good return on your investment.

That said, if you are marketing for higher-margin services—dental implants, orthodontics, cosmetic dentistry, laser dentistry, or sleep dentistry, for instance—you have to expect the acquisition costs to be higher. These are high-margin services, so there's typically more competition, and you might see acquisition costs of $300 to $700 for these types of patients. Ultimately, it's about ROI, so even if you had to spend $500 to acquire a patient for a $4,000 procedure, your ROI is quite good even after you subtract the costs for your materials, lab supplies, and so on.

My preference is to think about the lifetime value of a patient since this is really the best way to understand what an acceptable patient acquisition cost would be. This amount will obviously vary by practice and specialty, but the key is to work with your CPA to truly understand what an average patient is worth to you over time. For example, let's say you typically have around two thousand active patients each year, and your practice does $1 million in annual collections. This would equate to $500 per year for the average patient. If they stay with you for an average of four years, then you could calculate the lifetime value of a patient as $500 X 4 = $2,000. You could certainly develop a more complicated (and accurate) model that also factors in overhead and associated costs to determine the net value. Regardless, understanding what a patient is really worth to you helps put in perspective what you might be willing to spend to acquire them. Depending on your growth goals you may be willing to tolerate new patient acquisition costs in the $400-$500 range.

TRACKING BUSINESS PERFORMANCE

Now that we've reviewed how to track marketing performance, we can discuss the bigger picture, which is tracking overall business performance. As noted in section 1, mastering practice growth means all aspects of the business must be operating well and in harmony if the goal is to grow and increase profitability. Marketing alone is clearly not enough.

I always recommend practices use business analysis software to help summarize all the major KPIs. A good software program will have the ability to accurately track and clearly display important KPIs in all major categories such as new patient count, doctor utilization, hygiene utilization, doctor production, hygiene production, case acceptance percentage, average treatment plan recommended, patient retention rate, and other related metrics. Financial metrics are also important to review on a monthly basis.

As you scale, it is a good idea to utilize business analysis software that can effectively display data for multiple locations by region, state, and other categories. While there are many software solutions on the market, the best business analysis software I've seen is Practice Analytics.

PRACTICE ANALYTICS

Practice Analytics is a dental practice analysis software tool designed to help monitor and diagnose the business health of your dental practice. The software allows dentists, managers, consultants, and staff to quickly identify how they are performing using a real-time, cloud-based dashboard with KPIs.

Everyone in the office has responsibilities and job functions that can be measured. Practice Analytics uses the raw data found deep inside your practice management system to simplify and optimize your ability to manage the business more intelligently and effectively. The software focuses on three distinct modules: clinical, front office, and overall business. This provides the ability to quickly determine how different components of the practice are doing on performance relative to set goals and also allows for trend analysis over time.

Practice Analytics offers various levels of customization so practices can focus on the metrics they deem to be the most important. Likewise, for group practices and DSOs the software offers an easy-to-use navigation menu that allows the ability to view performance by practice, city, region, and doctor and staff.

SERVICE RECOMMENDATION: PRACTICE ANALYTICS

Practice Analytics is a dental practice analysis software tool designed to help monitor and diagnose the business health of your dental practice, allowing dentists, managers, consultants, and staff to quickly identify how they are performing using a real-time, cloud-based dashboard with KPIs.

For more information, please see section 6, "Recommended Resources to Grow Your Practice."

GROWING TO MULTIPLE LOCATIONS AND UP TO A DSO

"I'd like to build a larger group/DSO, but I'm not sure how to go about it— or even if it's the right choice for me."

"What advice would you give me?"

hear this question or variations on it all the time, as DSOs—dental support organizations—are becoming an ever more popular business model in the dental industry. Current estimates are that 20 to 25 percent of practices nationwide are already part of a DSO or group, and that number is continuing to grow at an impressive rate. There are powerful economic factors driving this consolidation, so most people predict the consolidation will continue for years to come.

My business partner at The DSO Project, Dr. Jeromy Dixson, is a general dentist and has a master of business administration (MBA). He has started, grown, and ultimately sold a sizable DSO himself, and his experience provides valuable insights into what it takes to build a successful DSO, so you'll be hearing from him throughout this section.

THE PROS AND CONS OF SCALING UP

Why would you want to consider scaling up from one or two locations to five, ten, or twenty locations? One compelling reason is financial: a doctor with multiple successful practices can potentially make far more money scaling than they ever could just by running one or two practices. Another reason is a sense of mission; we talk to many dentists who are passionate about delivering quality healthcare and who see scaling up as an opportunity to bring higher standards of treatment to more people.

A dental support organization also provides more efficient centralized services and support services to a practice so the dentist can focus on the clinical work, rather than having to handle HR, payroll, insurance, marketing, IT, finance, and all the other business aspects of running the practice.

That said, as Dr. Dixson points out, "There are a lot of people who want to build a group practice or a DSO for the wrong reasons. One of my mantras is 'people, product, profits'—and in that order. If you get the people part of it right and the product part right, then profits will flow from having those essential pillars in place. Some dentists want to grow but aren't doing it for the right reasons; they may lack an idea that would differentiate them from others, or they don't have a clear picture for the path forward."

From a financial point of view, there's never been a better time to scale up. A single practice will typically sell for about three to four times its EBITDA (earnings before interest, taxes, depreciation, and amortization), while even a smaller, well-functioning DSO of perhaps eight or ten locations will have a valuation multiple close to double what that valuation multiple would be per practice—and as the DSO grows, that valuation multiple can triple or even quadruple.

Why? One reason is the appeal DSOs have for institutional investors, private equity, and family offices (investment firms managed by wealthy families with their own funds) that see the value in consolidation and are eager to invest in dentistry as it becomes more consolidated. Second, the larger DSOs, backed by investors, are willing to pay to acquire high-quality small groups. What we see is that as small groups are built, the medium and large groups buy them up, especially those of exceptionally high quality.

What are the most important qualities we find in people who have successfully scaled a DSO? Certainly, it's not for everyone, and as Dr. Dixson notes:

I've personally seen many dentists set out on the difficult path of scaling into a DSO, but only a select few end up reaching or exceeding their initial goals. More often than not, after a few years of struggle, I hear a downtrodden owner with markedly less passion relay something similar to the sentiment, "I had no idea it would be so hard!" The traits I think are of critical importance include:

- visionary

- a broad skill set

- intellectually curious and a lifelong learner

- strong emotional intelligence and self-awareness

- collaborative since this can't be a one-person operation

- execution focused

- a polymath with expertise and experience in several different industries or niches—so if dentistry is all you know or want to know, this might not be for you

- a rainmaker, someone who is comfortable with networking, connecting, and reaching out to bring others into your practice, whether they're clinicians, executives, or the owners of a practice you're interested in acquiring

For instance, I'm a dentist: I went to dental school, went back to school for my MBA, got involved in the business end with leadership and management, and then got involved on the consulting side along with working with private equity investors—none of which are typical of a dentist's career path. That's true of those who I see having the most success in building DSOs. You've got to be invested in building your leadership and management toolbox. If an honest personal assessment tells you that you don't really have much enthusiasm for acquiring those kinds of skills, you're not likely to be successful in building a DSO.

START WITH A FIRM FOUNDATION: BUILDING YOUR DSO PRACTICE HOUSE

In explaining how a well-functioning DSO is created, Dr. Dixson finds it helpful to use this illustration to clarify his points:

In my experience, the framework of all successful DSOs is similar. All sustainably successful dental groups exhibit these critical components illustrated in the DSO house concept on the next page.

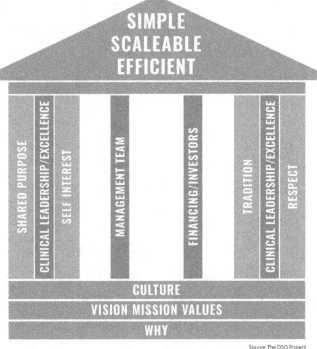

Source: The DSO Project

All structures rely on a solid foundation for stability, and a DSO is no different. The foundation of the DSO house is the organization's mission, vision, and values. As with any house, the foundation protects it from outside elements that will damage and slowly rot it over time.

Each of these—the mission, vision, and values—should be stated in as few words as possible and be so simply and clearly written that everyone in the organization can easily understand them. The mission will guide every decision as the DSO grows and scales. The vision must encapsulate the leader's plan for what the company will become as it scales. The values of the organization should be universal enough to guide how team members of the DSO act as they treat patients (and how they treat each other) at all times. This foundation is a gating item for all decisions within the organization so that if a proposed action does not align with the mission, vision, and values, it is not taken.

A good example of this concept are the mission, vision, and values of the DSO I built and led:

- Mission: Ultimate service. Superior performance. Positive impact.

- Vision: Transform oral healthcare.

- Value(s): Patients first.

The roof of the DSO house is another critical gating item as you build and scale a DSO. The roof of any house protects it from incursions by harmful outside elements such as rain, snow, ice, and wind. It allows the inside of the home to maintain a temperature independent of the outside to keep its inhabitants insulated from the elements. Asking whether any proposed action is simple, scalable, and efficient protects the organization from the "scaling of chaos," which often occurs when this roof concept is not firmly in place.

There are three key structural pillars associated with the DSO house: these are exceptional clinical quality and leadership, the right financing/investors, and a synergistic management team.

Exceptional clinical quality and leadership is self-explanatory and is a prerequisite to ensuring your DSO is built for the long haul. Secondary pillars support this idea, assisting in fully engaging the dentists who drive practice growth in ways that help to motivate and align their actions with organizational goals. These secondary pillars include building a shared purpose between the organization and the dentists, satisfying the self-interests of the dentists (including compensation and professional goals), ensuring full personal and professional respect of the dentists in every way possible, and creating a culture with traditions that are in alignment with the mutual goals of the dentists and the organization.

Having the right financing/investors is key to the growth curve of even the most well-conceived DSO. Emerging groups often rely on traditional banks to provide capital in the form of dental loans to fuel growth in the early stages. The idea is to use debt financing as long as possible so you can avoid giving up equity in these early stages. Indeed, there are a handful of banks that are focused on lending to dental groups so they can be very helpful in the early to mid stages of building your DSO. Over time, with size and scale, these resources can become limiting to the acceleration of the scaling process when it is time for the exponential growth phase to begin, and this is another reason why investors in the form of private equity firms or family offices can be a better fit when you're looking for growth capital. A good personality/cultural fit, a proper deal structure (minority/non-controlling, majority/controlling, etc.), and the ability to add clear value to the venture are the critical components to look for in investors in your organization. Many entrepreneurs find it difficult to know which investors are the best fit, what the proper deal structure ought to be, and what constitutes adding value as a partner.

The final key pillar is a synergistic management team. With some organizational scale, this often consists of the following positions and characteristics:

- CEO (chief executive officer): visionary, broad skills, curious, lifelong learner, strong emotional intelligence, self-awareness, collaborative, execution focused, polymath, and rainmaker

- COO (chief operating officer): bias toward action, process and systems focused, eye for talent, ambassadorial, and squashes drama

- CFO (chief financial officer)/Controller: strong financial skills and background, operational and clinical understanding, dental understanding/experience, and quick study

- CDO (chief dental officer): respected clinician and mentor, likable, strong integrity, aligned with business goals, and influencer

As you can see, not everyone has to be good at everything or strong in every personal quality—but they do have to be great at what's required of them both personally and professionally. Taking time to hire the right people for these key positions will save you headaches and money down the line. Experience has taught me that hiring the best advisors and paying them well isn't a luxury but a necessity because any other approach is a false economy that ends up costing you more. I've heard people say, "I don't want to pay $500 per hour for an attorney. I want to pay $200 per hour." But if you hire an attorney without the specific experience in this area who sets up your DSO incorrectly, then you're not saving money. You're actually hurting yourself and potentially creating a major mess—stepping over a quarter to get a nickel, as the saying goes.

Forming up the right team doesn't stop at the C-suite level, of course, because your frontline team and middle management also have to share your vision and sense of mission in the work they do with your patients every day. If your office manager isn't approaching every interaction with the mantra "patients first," you're not going to grow. Everyone needs to be committed to the wider organization, and that starts with getting the right people in the right jobs.

Even the most careful hiring processes can't completely eliminate the necessity for what I call "necessary endings," though, because human relations are complex and dynamic, and you can't always accurately predict how someone is going to work in a particular position. I've had people that were an issue within the organization; I tend to be empathetic toward people, and I want to see them succeed, and often, I have kept those people too long. But what I discovered was that when I have ultimately let them go, it's been a net positive for the organization, without fail. Whether it's a question of removing the toxicity from the organization or simply that the next person in the job is a better fit, overall having the "right people in the right seats" improves overall performance and morale. So do this sooner than later!

This gets more complex as you expand because your locations may be several miles or several hours apart. That's why your process must be deliberate; begin with the end in mind, and be proactive about how you're building it.

WHY DENTAL SUPPORT ORGANIZATIONS FAIL

There are many potential hazards you'll have to navigate in starting and scaling up your DSO. Some of these have to do with your personality type and strengths, while others, such as regulatory issues or recruitment, are external factors you need to weigh and address as you proceed.

Let's assume you've thought through your motivation and mission, you've got a clear vision for what you want to accomplish in scaling up, and you are sufficiently entrepreneurial in character to relish the challenges scaling up will certainly pose. All of that is good, but it's important to understand that it may not be enough. Dr. Dixson and I have spent enough time analyzing successes and failures in this arena to know that even with all these attributes, failure can happen.

When the culture is wrong, failure is almost guaranteed.

The foundational culture is another piece that can be neglected as you're scaling up, but success requires a culture of support for one another as peers and colleagues, as well as a commitment to the positive, service-oriented attitude of putting your patients first. When the culture is wrong, failure is almost guaranteed.

Other potential pitfalls may include the regulatory climate in your state. Some states and state dental boards have tried to shut down or freeze out DSOs, so having a good legal advisor or attorney who understands the regulations and can help you to properly structure your enterprise to meet their requirements is essential not only as you're starting up but also as you continue to grow and scale.

The good news is that nationally the regulatory environment has been getting more DSO friendly over time.

There are other factors too that we feel strongly influence your odds for success. Having a solid system for doctor recruitment and retention is really important. You don't want your DSO to be just a starting point for someone fresh out of dental school; you need to offer your new hires a viable career path that paints a picture of what they can achieve working with you and sets their expectations that this is a career destination. Offering them a clear route to equity and/or partnership, for instance, is certainly a powerful motivator.

Another key factor is having a good strategy for growth. In addition to a solid marketing plan and marketing partner such as WEO Media, you'll need to develop a plan for adding locations. That could mean sourcing and purchasing the right dental practices to bring into your group, starting out in a retail location, or finding a piece of land and either building out or starting your practice from scratch. When applicable, you'll want to make sure your site selection has favorable demographics and a good ratio of population to dentists.

GET A MENTOR—LEARN FROM OTHERS

Mentorship is another critical factor that can make or break your successful ramp up. Look to connect with others who have already gone down this path because the value of shared experience can't be overstated. One way to do that is to connect with peers who have been through the process. There's one group in particular, called

Dentist Entrepreneur Organization (DEO), that we feel is especially helpful to those starting the journey. DEO offers events and other resources to those looking to scale up.

If you've gone to their conferences and feel you're ready for a deeper dive, DEO offers mastermind groups; this is a smaller, more tight-knit community that gets together for educational events on a monthly basis and provides you with great content. It's a way to become part of a like-minded peer group in which you share best practices, refer each other to useful resources, and ask and answer one another's questions. DEO has done a great job of creating this community learning environment, and if you're starting a DSO, it's a tremendous resource.

In addition to getting involved in a learning community such as DEO, we also strongly advise engaging with a DSO coach with experience in the critical areas of starting and scaling a DSO or acquiring an existing one. This is exactly what Dr. Dixson and I have done, and it is reflected in the services offered by The DSO Project.

SERVICE RECOMMENDATION: THE DSO PROJECT

The DSO Project helps dentists develop, scale, and ramp up their groups, aiding them in properly structuring their DSO house from start-up to exit. We help dentists create solid business plans, find appropriate funding options for expansion, and connect with private equity for further scaling. We can develop a marketing program and metrics, create effective training programs for your staff, and build a great management team. Whether it's in creating the right kind of organizational culture or lining you up with the right law firm to properly structure your DSO, our coaching is hands on and based on expertise we've gained through our own experience as DSO owners, dental business owners, and executive consultants.

As you embark upon your group practice or DSO journey, partnering with coaches who have actually done it will exponentially increase your odds of success!

For more information about The DSO Project, please see section 6, "Recommended Resources to Grow Your Practice."

SERVICE RECOMMENDATION: DEO

The DEO is a peer-to-peer membership community of growth-minded dentist entrepreneurs working toward expanding their group practices. The DEO is a place where dentists are genuinely interested in each other's success—they share openly, and they support each other through the process of growing a managed group practice.

For more information, please see section 6, "Recommended Resources to Grow Your Practice."

DEMOGRAPHIC SITE SELECTION

Site selection is one of the most important factors that determines the likelihood of success for any dental practice. The ideal site for your next dental practice will have a ratio of population to dentists of at least two thousand to one or greater. There are several demographic service companies that can provide this type of analysis. One organization with excellent services in this area is REALscore. They provide a wide array of detailed analysis options to help dentists pick the best location available for their next practice, whether it be an acquisition or de novo.

SERVICE RECOMMENDATION: REALSCORE

REALscore provides practice location strategies for the entire dental industry by providing reports and consultation services for start-ups, existing practices, lenders, and distributors. These detailed reports include competition ratios, current and five-year forecast demographic information, and Location Search Reports to quickly and accurately discover locations or previously unknown pockets with the highest practitioner-to-population ratios.

For more information, please see section 6, "Recommended Resources to Grow Your Practice."

REAL ESTATE AND LEASE NEGOTIATIONS

Once you've selected your site (acquisition or de novo), the next step is dealing with the many details involved with real estate and lease negotiations. Healthcare real estate requires specialized knowledge and experience that is vastly different from common commercial real estate.

SERVICE RECOMMENDATION: CARR HEALTHCARE REALTY

Carr Healthcare is the nation's leading provider of commercial real estate services for healthcare tenants and buyers. Carr can handle every facet of your transaction, including purchase versus lease evaluation, lease analysis, and more.

For more information, please see section 6, "Recommended Resources to Grow Your Practice."

RECOMMENDED RESOURCES TO GROW YOUR PRACTICE

The preceding sections of this book have laid out in great detail the most important fundamentals for mastering practice growth. It starts with developing a great culture as well as operational and clinical excellence. A comprehensive marketing program is the next building block, which includes online and direct-to-consumer marketing. For some, their journey may involve growing to multiple locations or even a DSO. A solid system for tracking KPIs is absolutely essential to optimize clinical, operational, marketing, and financial performance.

This final section contains full-page summaries for all the recommended resource companies and organizations to help you in your journey. The companies are listed in alphabetical order for your ease of reference. I sincerely hope you will take advantage of the knowledge and resources contained in this book.

I wish you the best of luck in your pursuit of mastering practice growth!

ACADEMY OF DENTAL CPAS

The ADCPA was founded in 2001 to organize and share best practices among dental CPAs. Today there are dozens of ADCPA member firms collectively providing services to over nine thousand dentists across the country. This collective knowledge base is a powerful resource for any dentist looking to make good business decisions, minimize taxes, and maximize profitability.

WHY A DENTAL CPA?

A specialized CPA is your first and best line of defense in the often bewildering and sometimes challenging business world. A good dental CPA should also be one of your principal advisors on anything financial related within your dental practice.

Useful management reports and financial statements should be the beginning of the process, not the end. A skilled dental CPA will use ADCPA-approved reports like you use patients' scans and X-rays for evaluation, diagnosis, and treatment planning. The dental CPA analyzes such questions as, How is the financial health of my practice? What can I do now to minimize taxes next April? Is the office using best practices based on the dental CPA's knowledge of other successful offices? Is production appropriate for the number of personnel? Am I investing enough in marketing to grow my practice? Should I purchase new technology?

You want something more than a regular CPA—you want a business advisor, one who has specialized knowledge in dentistry. One who is proactive and forward thinking. To put it in accounting terms, you want an asset, not a liability.

CONTACT

Website: www.adcpa.org

CARECREDIT

For over thirty years, CareCredit has been providing a valuable financing option for treatments and procedures that typically are not covered by insurance or for times when insurance doesn't cover the full amount. CareCredit is also used by cardholders to pay for deductibles and copayments.

We think people like having financial options because that gives them the freedom to make decisions about treatment options so that they can do what's best for their situation and their family.

That's why CareCredit is here. We help make care possible today. CareCredit, from Synchrony, is one of the largest and most popular health, wellness, and beauty credit cards in the nation, serving millions of families each year. More than one hundred thousand enrolled dental teams accept CareCredit and more than twenty-eight million accounts have been opened since CareCredit began helping patients to get the care they need and want.

COMPANY SERVICES

- Patients or clients quickly apply in your practice, over the phone, or on their smart device—and get an instant credit decision.

- Once approved, they can immediately use the CareCredit credit card to pay for deductibles, copays, and coinsurance and costs not covered by insurance.

- Your practice gets paid within two business days, with no responsibility if the cardholder delays or defaults.

CONTACT
Website: www.carecredit.com
Phone: 800-300-3046

CARR HEALTHCARE REALTY

Carr Healthcare is the nation's leading provider of commercial real estate services for healthcare tenants and buyers. Healthcare real estate requires specialized knowledge and experience that is vastly different from common commercial real estate.

As your dental real estate experts, we handle every facet of your transaction, including site selection, purchase versus lease evaluation, lease analysis, and more. We recognize the importance of making sure every detail of your space and the economics line up with your specialty. We pay close attention to details, including the location and ergonomics of operatories, the laboratory, the sterilization area, and the consultation room and even technology use.

Our expert real estate services and skilled negotiating ensure you obtain the most favorable terms and concessions possible.

SPECIAL OFFER

Readers of this book are entitled to a free lease and real estate evaluation. This evaluation will determine where you stand in relationship to your current market and will give you the recommended timeline and process for maximizing the savings on your next lease renewal or purchase. Call or email us today.

CONTACT

Website: www.carr.us
Phone: 800-651-7284
Email: webform@carr.us

DEAR DOCTOR

Established by dentists in 2006, Dear Doctor is a patient education company providing a variety of products to grow dental practices and increase case acceptance. From videos for your website to dental office television and a chairside consultation product, the goal is to educate your patients, helping them make more informed decisions about their care.

Dear Doctor's products promote dentistry in a positive light and lead to positive oral health decisions, resulting in greater follow-through in scheduling appointments, increased inquiries about services, and ultimately greater case acceptance.

COMPANY SERVICES

- **Website video library.**

- **Dear Doctor TV.**

- **Consult Assistant.**

SPECIAL OFFER

Readers of this book are entitled to a risk-free, thirty-day trial of Dear Doctor TV, plus one free month of service. Call or email us today.

CONTACT

Website: www.deardoctor.com
Phone: 866-821-5458
Email: info@deardoctor.com

DEO: DENTIST ENTREPRENEUR ORGANIZATION

The DEO is a peer-to-peer membership community of growth-minded dentist entrepreneurs working toward expanding their group practices. The DEO is a place where dentists are genuinely interested in each other's success—they share openly, and they support each other through the process of growing a managed group practice.

DEO members will learn how to add locations, attract associates, and build a great business. As you scale, you'll also need access to some fundamental knowledge. You'll need to know how to find practices or locations to acquire, how to set up associate compensation models, how to develop a culture, and the basic tenets of building a great company. The DEO will give you access to these elements and more.

The DEO hosts comprehensive national conferences as well as smaller mastermind groups for more personalized learning and development.

SPECIAL OFFER

Readers of this book are entitled to $200 off event registration. To redeem, please contact us and use this code: **GROWTH-BOOK**.

CONTACT

Website: www.deodentalgroup.com
Phone: 503-427-9136
Email: dacopan@deodentalgroup.com

THE DSO PROJECT

The DSO Project is a unique coaching and advising firm offering dentists an opportunity to partner with industry experts who will assist them in their DSO journey. We coach dentists every step of the way from start-up through exit. We work with our clients in all critical areas for success including building the right culture, optimizing operations, DSO legal structure formation, business plan development, marketing plan development, building a management team, implementing management processes and KPIs, developing financing and equity funding options, and much more.

Our CEO, Jeromy Dixson (DMD, MBA), is the only dentist in the country who has founded, successfully scaled, and sold his DSO and is now coaching other dentists on how to do exactly what he did. Our president, Ian McNickle (MBA), is a dental industry veteran and has deep expertise in dental marketing, business management, operations, strategy, and scaling companies. Their combined experience tremendously increases the odds of success for dentist entrepreneurs building their DSOs.

SPECIAL OFFER

Readers of this book are entitled to a complimentary consultation with The DSO Project where we will advise you on your DSO goals and objectives. To redeem, please email us and use this code: **DSO-BOOK**.

CONTACT

Website: www.dsoproject.com
Email: info@dsoproject.com

FORTUNE MANAGEMENT

Fortune Management is the nation's largest and most comprehensive practice management organization. Our executive coaches are practice management specialists who will guide you and your team through the intricacies of practice ownership, team leadership, business management, and entrepreneurial success. From start-up to transition, whether you're in a rural market or a major metropolitan area, our expert coaches and training curriculum will provide you with the resources you and your team need to succeed.

COMPANY SERVICES

- **Executive coach.**
- **Practice management specialist.**
- **Key business strategist.**

SPECIAL OFFER

Readers of this book are entitled to a complimentary practice analysis and opportunity assessment of your practice by a Fortune Management executive coach ($2,500 value). To register for your complimentary assessment, please mention **Growth-Book** when you call or email us.

CONTACT

Website: www.fortunemgmt.com
Phone: 800-628-1052
Email: fortune@fortunemgmt.com

HARRIS BIOMEDICAL

Harris Biomedical is a full-service, one-stop, consulting firm that specializes in dental practice regulatory compliance for individual practices on up to large DSOs. We design and prepare OSHA and HIPAA written policy and procedure manuals and train your staff— all tailored to the activities of your individual dental practice based on the specific requirements of your city, county, and state.

We train your staff through in-service or live, interactive webinars and provide 24/7 support at no cost. And if you are ever cited, we will assist in your appeal process, forever, at no cost as long as you are our client.

Having prepared more than 8,000 OSHA/WISHA (Washington Industrial Safety and Health Act) and 5,500 HIPAA compliance programs for dental practices across the country and completed staff training for more than 200,000 dental care professionals since 1989, our one-stop approach to compliance is recognized as one of the dental industry's best.

SPECIAL OFFER

Readers of this book are entitled to a 15 percent discount on all services, including OSHA and HIPAA program manuals and staff training, and we will provide a free "self-assessment" facility review to every new client. Please contact us today and mention the discount code: **GROWTH-BOOK**.

CONTACT

Website: www.harrisbiomedical.net
Phone: 866-548-2468
Email: info@harrisbiomedical.net

KLEER

Kleer is an advanced, cloud-based platform that enables a dental practice to easily design and manage their own membership plan and offer it directly to their uninsured patients. Kleer is turnkey and *free* to implement and includes everything a practice needs to create and manage a successful membership plan.

For practices, it adds new, recurring revenue through patient subscription fees that go directly to the practice. For patients, Kleer membership plans provide a simple, comprehensive, and affordable dental care plan that enables them to take a proactive approach to managing their oral health.

COMPANY SERVICES

- **Patient landing page.**

- **Marketing support.**

- **Renewal support.**

- **Market research.**

- **Product innovation.**

SPECIAL OFFER

Kleer is *free* and easy to implement. There are no setup or monthly fees and no charges for marketing materials or support. We only get paid if you get paid. Book an online demo at www.kleer.com and get started today!

CONTACT

Website: www.kleer.com
Phone: 844-965-5337

NOBEL BIOCARE

Nobel Biocare is a market leader in offering solutions from root to tooth, covering dental implants; restorative components; individualized, patient-specific prosthetics; and biomaterials.

By providing you access to cutting-edge technology, growth tools, and training and education, Nobel Biocare enables you to chart your path to success and satisfied patients.

Nobel Biocare territory representatives offer an array of practice development and growth services and support to help your practice grow and increase implant patients.

- **NobelActive.**

- **All-on-4 Treatment Concept.**

- **NobelPearl.**

- **Trefoil.**

- **DTX Studio Software and X-Guide.**

SPECIAL OFFER

To learn more about how to incorporate dental implants into your practice or about the latest innovation in implant dentistry, please visit www.nobelbiocare.com/GrowthBook for a special introductory offer and to request a visit from a Nobel Biocare representative.

CONTACT

Website: www.nobelbiocare.com
Phone: 800-322-5001

PATIENT PRISM

Patient Prism is an award-winning solution to one of the biggest problems in dentistry: getting people to book an appointment. Offering software that quickly evaluates how staff handle phone calls from prospective patients, Patient Prism tracks, records, and coaches new patient phone calls using a combination of artificial intelligence, machine learning, and experienced dental call coaches.

When a potential patient ends the phone call without booking an appointment, Patient Prism sends an alert to the dental practice typically within an hour detailing what the caller wanted, why they didn't book, and effective phrasing the team can use to call back the patient and convert that lost opportunity into a booked appointment. In addition, there are literally dozens of reports, dashboards, and metrics to help you maximize your conversion rate and generate exceptional new patient flow.

COMPANY SERVICES

- **Rapid call analytics and coaching.**
- **Alerts.**
- **Track marketing effectiveness.**
- **Evaluate, coach, and develop the people who field your inbound calls.**
- **Manage progress with dashboards and reporting.**
- **Video training library.**

SPECIAL OFFER

Mention this book and save 10 percent with no setup or termination fees. Call us today.

CONTACT

Website: www.patientprism.com

Phone: 800-381-3638

PRACTICE ANALYTICS

Practice Analytics is a dental practice analysis software tool designed to help monitor and diagnose the business health of your dental practice, allowing dentists, managers, consultants, and staff to quickly identify how they are performing using a real-time, cloud-based dashboard with key performance indicators.

Practice Analytics uses the raw data found deep inside your practice management system to simplify and optimize your ability to manage the business effectively. The software focuses on three distinct modules: clinical, front office, and overall business. Practice Analytics offers various levels of customization so practices can focus on the metrics most important to them. For group practices and DSOs, the software offers easy-to-use navigation menus to analyze all practice locations in real time and over time.

COMPANY SERVICES

- **The Clinical Module.**
- **The Front Office Module.**
- **The Business Module.**

SPECIAL OFFER

Readers of this book are eligible to have their setup fee waived and monthly fees discounted up to 30 percent. To redeem this offer, please contact us and use this discount code: **GROWTH-BOOK**.

CONTACT

Website: www.practiceanalytics.com
Phone: 360-218-2497
Please visit our website to request a demo.

REALSCORE

REALscore provides practice location strategy for the entire dental industry by providing reports and consultation services for start-ups, existing practices, lenders, and distributors.

These detailed reports include competition ratios, current and five-year forecast demographic information, and Location Search Reports to quickly and accurately discover locations or previously unknown pockets with the highest practitioner-to-population ratios. Our world-class data comes from the best demographic and practitioner data providers in the country.

COMPANY SERVICES

- **REALscore Location Search Reports (LSRs)**
- **REALscore Demographic & Practitioner to Population Report (DPR).**
- **Complimentary consulting call.**

SPECIAL OFFER

Readers of this book are entitled to a 10 percent discount on all REALscore reports. Fill out the contact form on our Contact Us page, and we'll contact you to set up an appointment.

CONTACT

Website: www.realscore.com
Email: david.james@realscore.com

SIMPLIFEYE

Amplify is Simplifeye's live chat patient acquisition tool. It is a HIPAA-compliant web chat that sits on a practice's website and can be installed on any website. The chat is staffed by smile specialists, specifically trained in dental, and the service is operated 24/7 every day of the year. Amplify helps to convert website visitors into new patients through smile specialists who empathetically engage in chat conversations.

In addition to scheduling patients, Amplify helps a practice in a variety of ways. Staff time is saved due to reduced call volume, and search engine optimization is improved as the average time spent on the site increases.

Monitoring the ROI is extremely simple. Simplifeye provides a practice dashboard that clearly tracks the total and average chat time and illustrates the stage of each patient referral. These stages provide the front desk with enough information to increase conversion rates.

SPECIAL OFFER

Readers of this book can receive $50 off the retail price of Amplify.

CONTACT

Website: www.simplifeye.co
Phone: 646-846-7467
Email: sales@simplifeye.com

WEAVE

Weave offers a phone solution integrated with patient communication tools such as appointment reminders, providing personalized communication in an automated fashion. Weave increases efficiency by designing tools for ease of use and effective outcomes while assisting your team with smart, personalized automation, significantly reducing cancellations and missed calls and increasing appointments from both new and existing patients.

COMPANY SERVICES

- **Screen pop.**

- **Administration of team communication.**

- **Handling patient review requests.**

- **Missed call management.**

- **Schedule control.**

- **Weave app.**

SPECIAL OFFER

Readers of this book will receive 50 percent off the installation fee when they sign up for Weave! To redeem, please fill out the form at the following link: try.getweave.com/book/.

CONTACT

Website: www.getweave.com
Phone: 888-545-8880
Email: sdrs@getweave.com

WEO MEDIA— DENTAL MARKETING

WEO Media is a full-service dental marketing agency providing dentists with a wide range of services to market and grow their practices. WEO Media consultants work with clients to understand their unique needs, goals, competition, and budget in order to provide customized marketing solutions for their practices.

WEO Media has won the dental industry's top award four years in a row for websites and online marketing—the Cellerant Best of Class Technology Award, which is presented every year at the annual American Dental Association conference. WEO Media services over seven hundred practices nationwide.

COMPANY SERVICES

- Websites (secure, responsive)
- SEO (search engine optimization)
- PPC (pay-per-click) ad campaigns
- Social media
- Online reputation management
- Custom video production
- Patient education website videos
- Photo shoots
- Online appointment scheduling
- Online patient forms
- Premium Healthgrades profiles

- Direct mail campaigns

- Branding and graphic design

- Strategy development

- Patient email newsletters

- Call tracking and recording

SPECIAL OFFER

Readers of this book are entitled to a *free* marketing consultation and 10 percent off marketing service setup fees. To redeem, when you call or email us, please use this code: **GROWTH-BOOK**.

CONTACT

Website: www.weomedia.com
Phone: 888-246-6906
Email: info@weomedia.com

ABOUT THE AUTHOR

Ian McNickle is a serial entrepreneur, having successfully founded and scaled several companies. Ian is a cofounder of and partner at WEO Media, a four-time "Best of Class," award-winning dental marketing firm. Under his leadership, WEO Media has grown quickly to become one of the most widely respected dental marketing firms in North America and has garnered an impressive list of industry endorsements and awards. He is also a partner at and the president of The DSO Project, a national consultancy advising dentists on how to start, optimize, scale, fund, and successfully exit a dental support organization.

Ian is a nationally recognized marketer, writer, and public speaker. He has developed significant expertise in all aspects of dental marketing (online and direct to consumer), growth strategy, business development, business operations, and related topics. In 2019 Ian was named a top continuing education (CE) leader by *Dentistry Today*.

Ian lectures all over North America at dental conferences, study clubs, and dental societies and conducts numerous seminars and webinars. His teaching style breaks down the complexities of dental marketing into an easy-to-understand approach that the nonmarketer can comprehend and implement. Ian has written articles for numerous industry publications including *Dental Products Report*, *The Progressive Dentist*, and many other industry publications.

Prior to his work with WEO Media and The DSO Project, Ian worked in the high-tech industry for ten years in various engineering and management positions at Siltronic and Xerox. He left high tech in 2006 and cofounded a regional marketing consulting firm that he ran for several years before eventually cofounding WEO Media in 2009.

Ian has a bachelor of science in mechanical engineering from Washington State University, where he was also a graduate of the University Honors Program. In addition, he graduated cum laude with a master of business administration from the University of Washington.

Ian is an avid endurance athlete, having completed dozens of marathon, ultramarathon, and Ironman triathlon events. His favorite activity is simply spending time with his wife, Andrea, and three children Evelyn, Morgan, and Brendan. This book is dedicated to them.

CPSIA information can be obtained
at www.ICGtesting.com
Printed in the USA
JSHW021809111019
1887JS00003B/5